COLLECTIONS

A Harcourt Reading / Language Arts Program

Oh good, you're here!

You're just in time.

JUST IN TIME

Harcourt

Orlando   Boston   Dallas   Chicago   San Diego

COLLECTIONS

A Harcourt Reading / Language Arts Program

JUST IN TIME

SENIOR AUTHORS

Roger C. Farr • Dorothy S. Strickland • Isabel L. Beck

AUTHORS

Richard F. Abrahamson • Alma Flor Ada • Bernice E. Cullinan • Margaret McKeown • Nancy Roser
Patricia Smith • Judy Wallis • Junko Yokota • Hallie Kay Yopp

SENIOR CONSULTANT

Asa G. Hilliard III

CONSULTANTS

Karen S. Kutiper • David A. Monti • Angelina Olivares

Harcourt

Orlando   Boston   Dallas   Chicago   San Diego

Visit *The Learning Site!*
www.harcourtschool.com

JUST IN TIME

Dear Reader,

Have you ever dreamed of solving a mystery? Have you ever thought of flying to visit the planets in a spaceship? Have you ever wished you could have a dinosaur as a pet?

In **Just in Time**, you will meet characters who have fun with their family and friends, travel near and far, and use their imaginations.

You are just in time for some good reading! Read on!

Sincerely,

The Authors

The Authors

Imagine That!

CONTENTS

3

The Park Bench
Fumiko Takeshita · Mamoru Suzuki

Good-bye, Curtis
by KEVIN HENKES
PICTURES BY MARISABINA RUSS

MAX FOUND TWO STICKS
BRIAN PINKNEY

ANTHONY REYNOSO: BORN TO Rope
BY MARTHA COOPER & GINGER GORDON

THEME
Neighborhood News

4

CONTENTS

THEME

TRAVEL TIME

CONTENTS

6

Using Reading Strategies

A strategy is a plan for doing something well.

You can use strategies when you read to help you understand a story better. First, look at the title and pictures. Then, think about what you want to find out. Using strategies like these can help you become a better reader.

Look at the list of strategies on page 9. You will learn how to use these strategies as you read the stories in this book. As you read, look back at the list to remind yourself of the strategies good readers use.

- Look for Words You Know
- Look at Word Bits and Parts
- Self-Correct
- Read Ahead
- Reread Aloud
- Use Picture Clues to Confirm Meaning
- Make and Confirm Predictions
- Sequence Events/Summarize
- Create Mental Images
- Use Context to Confirm Meaning
- Reread
- Make Inferences

Here are some ways to make sure you understand what you are reading:

✔ Copy the list of strategies onto a piece of construction paper.

✔ Fold it and use it as a bookmark as you read.

✔ After you read, talk with a classmate about the strategies you used.

Imagine That!

CONTENTS

Reader's Choice

There's a Dragon in My Sleeping Bag
by James Howe
FANTASY

Alex's brother has an imaginary friend—a dragon—that always takes Alex's space. Then Alex creates an imaginary friend of his own.

Award-Winning Author
READER'S CHOICE LIBRARY

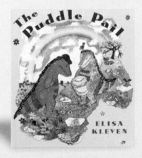

The Puddle Pail
by Elisa Kleven
FICTION

When Ernst and his brother decide to collect things, Ernst makes an unusual choice.

***SLJ* Best Book**
READER'S CHOICE LIBRARY

Regards to the Man in the Moon
by Ezra Jack Keats
FANTASY

With help from their imagination, Louie and his friends travel through space.

Award-Winning Author

Author: A True Story
by Helen Lester
AUTOBIOGRAPHY

Helen Lester writes about her life and how she started making children's books.

***SLJ* Best Book**

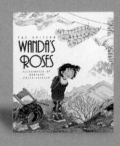

Wanda's Roses
by Pat Brisson
REALISTIC FICTION

Wanda thinks a thornbush is a rosebush. She begins caring for it every day, even though no roses bloom.

The Day Jimmy's

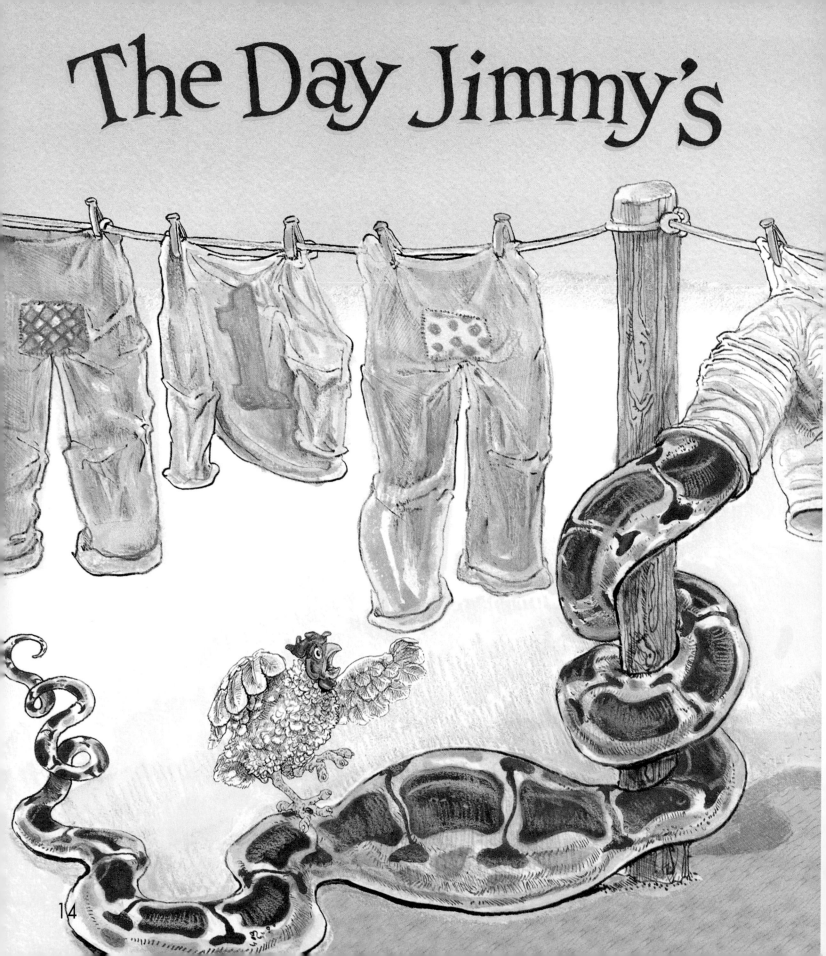

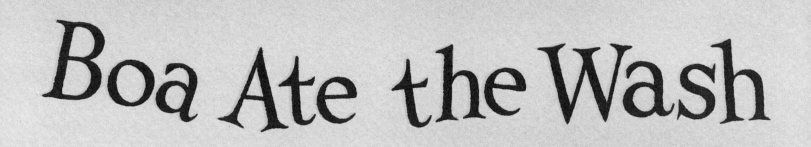

Boa Ate the Wash

ALA Notable
Children's Choice

by Trinka Hakes Noble   pictures by Steven Kellogg

"How was your class trip to the farm?"
"Oh . . . boring . . . kind of dull . . .
until the cow started crying."

"A cow . . . crying?"
"Yeah, you see, a haystack fell on her."
"But a haystack doesn't just fall over."

17

"It does if a farmer crashes into it with
his tractor."
"Oh, come on, a farmer wouldn't do that."
"He would if he were too busy yelling at
the pigs to get off our school bus."

18

"What were the pigs doing on the bus?"
"Eating our lunches."
"Why were they eating your lunches?"

19

"Because we threw their corn at each other, and they didn't have anything else to eat."

"Well, that makes sense, but why were you throwing corn?"

"Because we ran out of eggs."
"Out of eggs? Why were you throwing eggs?"

"Because of the boa constrictor."
"THE BOA CONSTRICTOR!"
"Yeah, Jimmy's pet boa constrictor."
"What was Jimmy's pet boa constrictor
doing on the farm?"

22

"Oh, he brought it to meet all the farm animals, but the chickens didn't like it."
"You mean he took it into the hen house?"
"Yeah, and the chickens started squawking and flying around."
"Go on, go on. What happened?"

"Well, one hen got excited and laid an egg, and it landed on Jenny's head."

"The hen?"

"No, the egg. And it broke—yucky—all over her hair."

"What did she do?"

"She got mad because she thought Tommy threw it, so she threw one at him."

"What did Tommy do?"

"Oh, he ducked and the egg hit Marianne in the face.

"So she threw one at Jenny but she missed and hit Jimmy, who dropped his boa constrictor."

"Oh, and I know, the next thing you knew, everyone was throwing eggs, right?"

"Right."

"And when you ran out of eggs, you threw the pigs' corn, right?"

"Right again."

25

"Well, what finally stopped it?"

"Well, we heard the farmer's wife screaming."

"Why was she screaming?"

"We never found out, because Mrs. Stanley made us get on the bus, and we sort of left in a hurry without the boa constrictor."

"I bet Jimmy was sad because he left his
pet boa constrictor."
"Oh, not really. We left in such a hurry
that one of the pigs didn't get off the bus,
so now he's got a pet pig."

"Boy, that sure sounds like an exciting trip."
"Yeah, I suppose, if you're the kind of kid
who likes class trips to the farm."

Think About It

1. What kinds of trouble does the class get into on the trip to the farm?

2. Would you like to take a class trip to a farm? Why or why not?

3. How would the story be different if the author did not have Jimmy bring his boa to the farm?

Meet the Author

Trinka Hakes Noble

Trinka Hakes Noble grew up on a small farm in Michigan. She went to a school that had only one room. In fact, she was the only person in her grade. Trinka Hakes Noble was an art teacher before she began writing and illustrating children's books. For "The Day Jimmy's Boa Ate the Wash," however, she wanted an illustrator with a style different from her own.

Meet the Illustrator

Steven Kellogg

Before Steven Kellogg illustrates a story, he reads the author's words carefully. He likes to picture the events in his head like a movie. Then he thinks of drawings that will show things the words don't tell. "Putting the words and pictures together is like a puzzle," he says. "That's the thing I like best about making children's books."

 Visit *The Learning Site!*
www.harcourtschool.com

by Katy Hall and
Lisa Eisenberg

SNAKEY

How did the boa
constrictor sign his
letter to the goat?

"With lots of hugs..."

In what river are you
sure to find snakes?

The Hississippi!

RIDDLES

*pictures by
Simms Taback*

What do snakes put on their kitchen floors?

Rep-tiles!

Why did the second-grade snakes get into trouble in school?

They were always hiss-pering!

Response Activities

Snake Cards Make fact cards

You can make snake trading cards.

1. Find out about boa constrictors and other snakes.
   Look for facts about snakes in your science book or in an
   encyclopedia.

2. Write each fact on an index card.

3. On the back of each card, draw a picture about the fact.

Trade your snake cards with classmates.

Snakes are
reptiles

News Flash from the Farm!

Perform a skit

What if a TV news reporter were at the farm the day Jimmy's boa got loose? Act out a skit of the reporter asking the story characters questions.

1. Decide who will be the news reporter and who will be each character.

2. Plan what everyone will say. Work together to write the questions the reporter will ask. Write each character's answers.

3. Practice your skit.

Perform your skit for others.

How I Spent My

Summer Vacation

written and illustrated
by Mark Teague

Parents' Choice

When summer began, I headed out west.
My parents had told me I needed a rest.
"Your imagination," they said, "is getting too wild.
It will do you some good to relax for a while."
So they put me aboard a westbound train
to visit Aunt Fern in her house on the plains.

How I Spent
My Summer
Vacation
By Wallace Bleff

SOUTHWEST

39

But I was captured by cowboys,
a wild-looking crowd.
Their manners were rough
and their voices were loud.

"I'm trying to get to my aunt's house," I said. But they carried me off to their cow camp instead.

The Cattle Boss growled, as he told me to sit,

"We need a new cowboy. Our old cowboy quit.

We could sure use your help. So what do you say?"

I thought for a minute, then I told him, "Okay."

Then I wrote to Aunt Fern, so she'd know where I'd gone.

I said not to worry, I wouldn't be long.

Dear Aunt,
Captured by
Cowboys. Don't
Worry. See
You soon.
Love,
Wallace

Aunt Fern
P.O. Box 5
Prairie
Tumblewe

That night I was given a new set of clothes.

Soon I looked like a wrangler from my head to my toes.

But there's more to a cowboy than boots and a hat,

I found out the next day

and the day after that.

Each day I discovered
some new cowboy
tricks.
From roping
and riding

to making fire with sticks.
Slowly the word spread
all over the land:
"That wrangler 'Kid Bleff'
is a first-rate cowhand!"

45

The day finally came when the roundup was through.
Aunt Fern called: "Come on over. Bring your
cowboys with you."
She was cooking a barbecue that very same day.
So we cleaned up (a little) and we headed her way.

The food was delicious. There was plenty to eat.
And the band that was playing just couldn't be beat.

But suddenly I noticed a terrible sight.

The cattle were stirring and stamping with fright.

It's a scene I'll remember till my very last day.

"They're gonna stampede!" I heard somebody say.

Just then they came charging. They charged right at *me!*

I looked for a hiding place—a rock, or a tree.

What I found was a tablecloth spread out on the ground.
So I turned like a matador
and spun it around.
It was a new kind of cowboying, a fantastic display!
The cattle were frightened and stampeded . . . away!

Then the cowboys all cheered, "Bleff's a true buckaroo!"
They shook my hand and slapped my back,
and Aunt Fern hugged me, too.

And *that's* how I spent my summer vacation.

I can hardly wait for show-and-tell!

Think About It

1. How does Wallace use his imagination in his report?

2. Which part of this story do you like the best? Why?

3. Why do you think the author shows the animals in the classroom at the end of the story?

52

Meet the Author and Illustrator

Mark Teague

What does Mark Teague do during *his* summer vacations? He spends most summers—and falls, winters, and springs—writing and illustrating children's books.

Mark Teague began making children's books while working at a bookstore in New York City. The children's books in the store reminded him of how much he enjoyed writing and illustrating his own stories when he was young.

 Visit *The Learning Site!* www.harcourtschool.com

Response Activities

Summer Song Make up a song

Work with a group to make up a song about things to do during summer vacation.

1. Sit on chairs in a circle.

2. Make up a rhythm for your song. Clap your hands and tap your feet.

3. Now say these words to your rhythm:
   What do we do in the summertime?

4. Go around the circle. Each person names one thing to do in the summer while everybody claps and taps the rhythm.

   We go swimming in the summertime.

Each person tries to add something new!

My Great Adventure Create a postcard

Wallace sends Aunt Fern a postcard. Make a postcard to send to Wallace.

1. On a sheet of paper, draw a picture of a place you would like to visit.

2. Turn your paper over. Draw a line down the middle.

3. Write a note to Wallace on the left side. Tell him about where you are and what you are doing. Make it sound exciting!

4. Make up an address for Wallace on the right side, and draw a stamp in the corner.

Dear Wallace,
Can You guess what I am doing at the beach? I am deep-sea diving for sunken treasure.
Your friend,
Susan

Wallace Bleff
121 Elm Street
Sunnyd

20¢

Context Clues for Word Meaning

Sometimes when you read, you find new words you do not understand. You can try to figure out the meaning of a new word by reading the words and sentences around it. Pictures can also give you clues.

Reread these sentences from "How I Spent My Summer Vacation":

> **That night I was given a new set of clothes. Soon I looked like a wrangler from my head to my toes.**

What does the word *wrangler* mean?

wrangler?   wrangler?   wrangler?

The next sentence in the story gives you a good clue.

But there's more to a cowboy than boots and a hat, ...

This sentence tells you something about a cowboy. You read that the new set of clothes is boots and a hat. The picture on page 44 also gives you a good clue. Wallace is dressed like a cowboy. The sentence and picture help you figure out that *wrangler* means "cowboy."

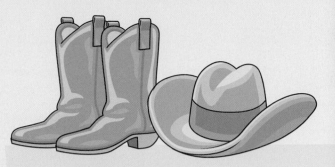

When you see a word you don't understand, look for clues in the other words and sentences you are reading and in the pictures.

WHAT HAVE YOU LEARNED?

Reread page 49 of "How I Spent My Summer Vacation." Find the word *stampede*.

1 What is the meaning of this word in the story?

2 What clues helped you figure out the meaning?

 Visit *The Learning Site!* www.harcourtschool.com

TRY THIS • TRY THIS • TRY THIS

Work with a partner to find another new word in the story. Talk about the words, sentences, and pictures that give you clues about the word's meaning.

Childrens'
Choice

Outstanding
Science
Trade Book

58

Dear Mr. Blueberry

story and pictures by SIMON JAMES

Dear Mr. Blueberry,

    I love whales very much and I think I saw one in my pond today. Please send me some information on whales, as I think he might be hurt.

Love
Emily

61

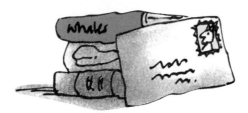

Dear Emily,

Here are some details about whales. I don't think you'll find it was a whale you saw, because whales don't live in ponds, but in salt water.

Yours sincerely
Your teacher,

Mr. Blueberry

Dear Mr. Blueberry,

I am now putting salt into the pond every day before breakfast and last night I saw my whale smile. I think he is feeling better.

Do you think he might be lost?

Love
Emily

Dear Emily,

Please don't put any more salt in the pond. I'm sure your parents won't be pleased.

I'm afraid there can't be a whale in your pond, because whales don't get lost, they always know where they are in the oceans.

Yours sincerely,

Mr. Blueberry

Dear Mr. Blueberry,

Tonight I am very happy because I saw my whale jump up and spurt lots of water. He looked blue.

Does this mean he might be a blue whale?

Love
Emily

P.S. What can I feed him with?

67

Dear Emily,

Blue whales are blue and they eat tiny shrimplike creatures that live in the sea. However, I must tell you that a blue whale is much too big to live in your pond.

Yours sincerely,

Mr. Blueberry

P.S. Perhaps it is a blue goldfish?

Dear Mr. Blueberry,

Last night I read your letter to my whale. Afterward he let me stroke his head. It was very exciting.

I secretly took him some crunched-up cornflakes and bread crumbs. This morning I looked in the pond and they were all gone!

I think I shall call him Arthur. What do you think?

Love
Emily

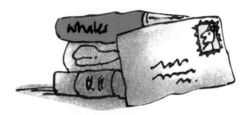

Dear Emily,

I must point out to you quite forcibly now that in no way could a whale live in your pond. You may not know that whales are migratory, which means they travel great distances each day.

I am sorry to disappoint you.

Yours sincerely,

Mr. Blueberry

Dear Mr. Blueberry,

Tonight I'm a little sad. Arthur has gone. I think your letter made sense to him and he has decided to be migratory again.

Love
Emily

Nantucket

August 20

Massachusetts

Dear Emily,

Please don't be too sad, it really was impossible for a whale to live in your pond. Perhaps when you are older you would like to sail the oceans studying and protecting whales.

Yours sincerely,

Mr. Blueberry

Dear Mr. Blueberry,

It's been the happiest day!
I went to the beach and you'll
never guess, but I saw Arthur!
I called to him and he smiled.
I knew it was Arthur because
he let me stroke his head.

I gave him some of my
sandwich and then we said
good-bye.

I shouted that I loved him
very much and, I hope you
don't mind . . .

I said you loved him, too.

Love
Emily (and Arthur)

Think About It

1 What are some things that Emily learns about whales?

2 Would you like to have a whale for a pet? Why or why not?

3 How would this story be different if Emily had seen a goldfish in her pond instead of a whale?

Meet the Author and Illustrator

Simon James

Simon James used to be a farmer. He was also a salesperson, a restaurant manager, and a police officer. In fact, Simon James has had fourteen different jobs! Now he makes children's books and teaches at a school near his house. He likes to show children how to have fun making a mess and showing their ideas at the same time.

Visit *The Learning Site!*
www.harcourtschool.com

A Whale Scale

A male narwhal grows a long tusk. This tusk is really an enormous tooth!

Baby killer whales are born black with yellow markings. As they grow, their yellow spots turn white like their parents'.

Humpback whales make noises that sound like songs.

0   10   20   30   40   50   60

Length in Feet

Right whales have no teeth.
They eat by swimming with
their mouths wide open
through large groups of tiny
animals and plants.

The blue whale is bigger than the
biggest dinosaur was. It can live for
about 80 years.

In "Dear Mr. Blueberry,"
Emily finds out that a blue
whale is much too big to
live in her pond. Read
about whales of all sizes on
this "whale of a scale."

Think About It
How are all these kinds
of whales alike?

70   80   90   100

81

Response Activities

Write Back Soon! Write a letter

1. Imagine that Emily sees another animal in her yard. What animal does she see?

2. Work with a partner to choose an animal. Find some facts about the animal in your science book or in an encyclopedia.

3. Write a letter to your partner about the new animal. One of you can be Mr. Blueberry. The other can be Emily.

Give your letter to your partner to read.

Dear Mr. Blueberry,
... a giraffe
... ackyard. He
... ry tall and has
... long neck. Why
... do giraffes have such

Dear Emily,
Giraffes have long necks so that they can eat leaves from tall trees.

Pet Books Make a booklet

Emily's whale would make an interesting pet. What animals would you like as pets? Make a book about pets.

1. On a sheet of paper, draw a picture of an animal that you think would make a good pet.

2. Finish this sentence and write it below the picture:

   _____ **would make a good pet because** _____.

3. Draw and write three or four pages for your book.

4. Make a book cover. Write a title for your book on the cover.

5. Staple the pages together.

Share your pet book with classmates.

My Pet Monkey
By Sarah

A Horse Is
A Great Pet
By Rob

All About
My Dog
By Erin

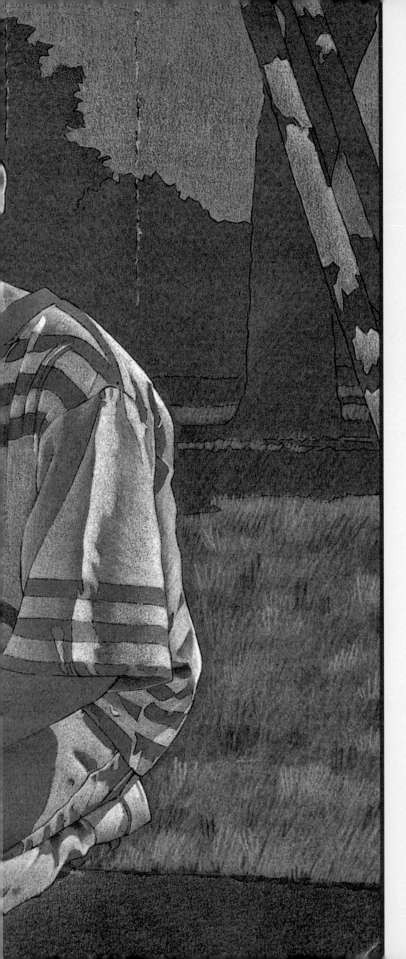

It's Probably Good
DINOSAURS
Are Extinct

by Ken Raney

I love dinosaurs. In fact,
I love dinosaurs so much
that I have always thought
I'd like to have one for a pet.
But when I really think
about it—it's probably good
that dinosaurs are extinct.

Just imagine how different
the world would be if
dinosaurs were alive today.
Think how big the zoo
would have to be.

A drive in the country
would come to a sudden
(and long) halt if a herd
of apatosaurus wanted to
cross the road.

87

And there would be more than dolphins and sea gulls to watch on a trip to the beach.

The world's most famous places would certainly look different if dinosaurs still roamed the earth. There might be pterosaurs at the pyramids.

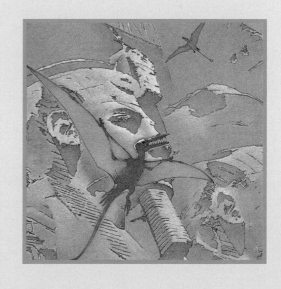

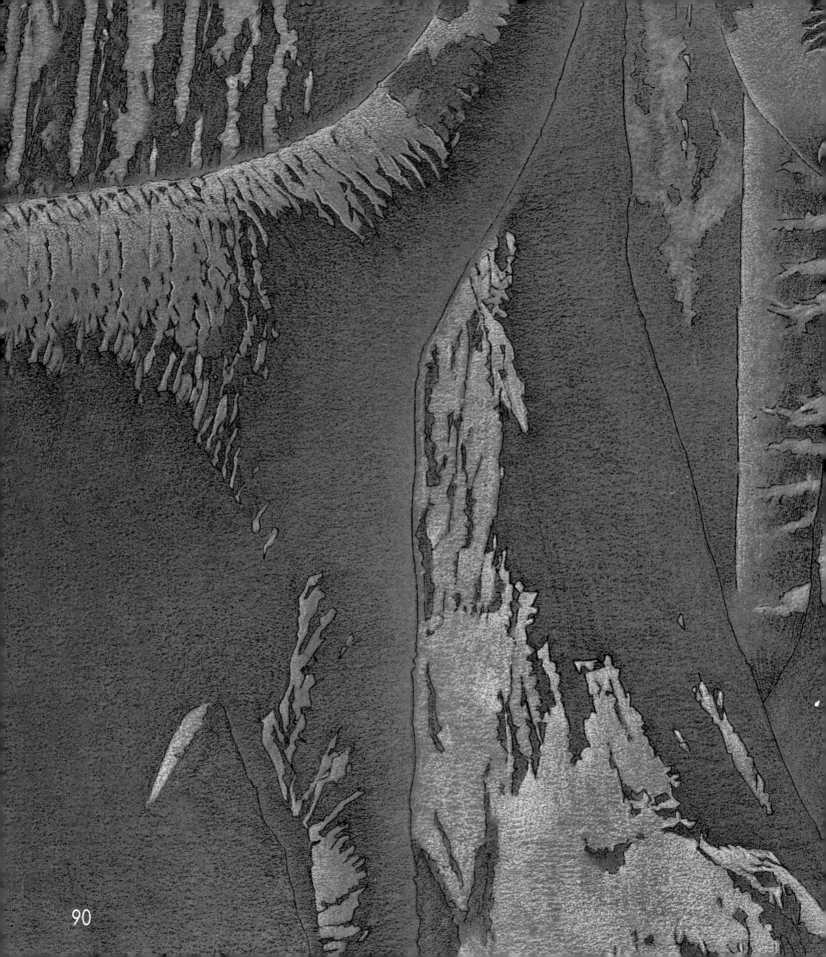

And at Redwood National Forest, the brachiosaurs would be nearly as tall as the trees.

91

History would be very different if dinosaurs had not become extinct . . .

What a sight it would have been to see a stegosaurus hitched to a covered wagon in the Old West.

Can you imagine how difficult some jobs would be if dinosaurs still existed? It would take real courage to be a paperboy.

BEWARE
OF
DINO

And a rodeo cowboy wouldn't want to get bucked off a protoceratops!

And can you imagine what it would be like to be a veterinarian?

Still, dinosaurs could be very useful for some things. In a parade, apatosaurus would always attract a crowd . . .

But, most of all, if dinosaurs were still around, think how much moms and dads would dread hearing: "Can I keep him . . . please?"

So I guess, all in all, it's probably good that dinosaurs are extinct.

Think About It

1 What would life be like if dinosaurs still roamed the earth?

2 What do you like most and least about this story?

3 Do you think dinosaurs would really act the way they do in this story? Explain your answer.

Meet the Author and Illustrator: Ken Raney

Ken Raney began drawing when he was six years old. He says, "I'm just a big kid myself — I write and illustrate the things that would have fascinated me as a child." Ken Raney lives in Kansas with his wife and four children.

Visit *The Learning Site!*
www.harcourtschool.com

RESPONSE ACTIVITIES

DINO RHYMES Write a poem

Write a poem about dinosaurs following you around. Use rhyming sentences like these:

Dinosaurs are here.

A _____ is near.

It's _____ behind the school.

It's drinking from my pool.

Choose a way to share your poem. Try an accordion book.

Dinosaur Village

Make a model

Work with a group to make a dinosaur village.

You will need:

clay   rocks   leaves   construction paper   scissors

1. Each group member chooses a dinosaur to make from clay.

2. Work together to plan where your dinosaurs will live. Use stones, leaves, and other objects to make the village. You can cut trees and big rocks out of construction paper.

3. Invite other groups to look at your dinosaur village. Tell them about each dinosaur that lives in it.

"**I**t's Probably Good Dinosaurs Are Extinct" is a make-believe, or fantasy, story. The story events could not happen in real life because dinosaurs are not alive anymore.

Think about the ways a make-believe story is different from a story that could happen in real life. In a real-life story, the events are things that could really happen.

Read the story events in this chart. Think about whether each event could happen in real life.

A herd of apatosaurus crosses the road.

A stegosaurus pulls a covered wagon.

A cowboy rides a protoceratops.

A herd of cows crosses the road.

A horse pulls a covered wagon.

A cowboy rides a bull.

The events on the right side of the chart could happen in real life, but the events on the left side could not.

When you read a story, ask yourself if it could happen in real life or if it is make-believe. This will help you understand the story better.

WHAT HAVE YOU LEARNED?

1 Reread pages 88 and 89 of "It's Probably Good Dinosaurs Are Extinct." Could the things that you see on these pages really happen? Explain your answer.

2 Look back at "Dear Mr. Blueberry." Would it be a real-life story or a make-believe story if Emily kept a goldfish instead of a whale in her pond? Explain your answer.

TRY THIS • TRY THIS • TRY THIS

Look back at some other stories that you have read. Think about the things that happened in each story. Make a list of real-life stories and a list of make-believe stories. Tell a partner why the stories on your lists are real-life or make-believe.

 Visit *The Learning Site!*
www.harcourtschool.com

109

cool

written and illustrated
by Nancy Poydar

Ali loved to draw.
She drew all the time.

One summer day, her mother said, "Ali, Ali, it's just too hot to be indoors!"

That's when Ali took her box of fat chalk outside.

It hadn't rained in weeks, so Ali drew grasses and flowers on the sidewalk. She was so busy she didn't notice other people coming out of the hot building. Some complained about the temperature. Some made newspaper fans.

The babies fussed. No one could get their mind off the heat.

Then, Ali drew a little lake
around Mrs. Frye's chair.
"My!" sighed Mrs. Frye as
she kicked off her sandals
and wiggled her toes.
"My, my!"

"Cool," piped up Ira Baker,
squinting in the sunlight.

That was when Ali drew the beach umbrella over Ira's head. "Cool!" he said again.

Mr. Boyle put down his newspaper fan and looked around to see what was so cool on such a hot day.

There was no more room in the lake or under the beach umbrella.

Mr. Boyle looked into the hot haze and complained, "Not even a breeze, not even a breeze."

That was when Ali drew the North Wind.

Mr. Boyle's teeth began to chatter. "Brrr," he said.

"Brrr," mimicked the babies. "Brrr, brrr!"

Ali drew a polar bear with pale yellow fur.

"Grrr," he seemed to say. "Grrr, grrr!"

"Wheee," squealed the babies as they took
turns riding on his back. "Wheee!"

"What a day," said Ali's mother, finally coming out of the hot building. "What a day!" she said when she saw what Ali had done! Then, she tested the water, admired the beach umbrella, bowed before the North Wind, and stayed out of the polar bear's way.

"Ali, soon you'll have everything covered!" she cried.

That was when Ali got the coolest idea of all.

She began by drawing little snow dots on the wall and the sidewalk, little snow dots around the big feet and little feet . . .

. . . little snow dots all over the lake and the beach umbrella. She drew polar bear paw prints and icicles, too.

She drew and she drew and she drew.

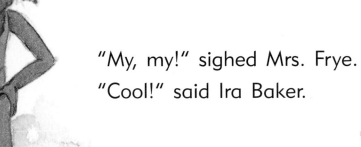

"My, my!" sighed Mrs. Frye.
"Cool!" said Ira Baker.

"Brrr!" chattered Mr. Boyle.
"Wheee!" squealed the babies.
"OOOO!" said the gathering crowd,
thrilled to be chilled to the bone!

No wonder no one noticed a little breeze rippling the haze and turning the leaves inside out. No wonder no one noticed the darkening sky or the first big drops of cold rain.

No one noticed until it pinged on the porches, drummed on the mailbox at the curb, and hissed off the hot sidewalk.

Then, it poured. Mrs. Frye did a jig with Mr. Boyle. The babies opened their mouths to catch the rain, and Ira Baker splashed in the first puddles that formed.

Only Ali noticed the sidewalk pictures blotch, dribble, and stream brightly into the rushing gutter.

Raging blizzard, polar bear, North Wind, beach umbrella, and little lake all washed away.

"Oh, no," Ali moaned. "Oh, no!"

But the crowd noticed Ali, whose drawing beat the heat.

They clapped, they cheered, and they lifted
her onto the tallest shoulders.
"Ali, Ali!" they chanted.

Ali loved to draw. She drew all the time.
Sometimes it was just too wet to draw outdoors.

Think About It

1 How does Ali's imagination help her neighbors beat the heat?

2 What would you draw to make the neighbors feel cool? Why?

3 What do you think Ali might do if it rains for a long time?

Meet the Author and Illustrator
Nancy Poydar

When she is not illustrating her own stories, Nancy Poydar likes to illustrate the stories of other well-known children's authors. She illustrated *The Adventures of Sugar and Junior*, by Angela Shelf Medearis.

Before she began making children's books, Nancy Poydar was a teacher. She lives in Massachusetts with her husband, her cat, Sunny, and her dog, Coco.

 Visit *The Learning Site!*
www.harcourtschool.com

Nancy Poydar

COol It!

by Lynn O'Donnell

Take This HOT Animal Quiz

When things heat up, these animals know how to cool down! Like humans, animals need to maintain a stable body temperature. If they overheat, their bodies might shut down.

We've listed three possible ways each of these animals keeps cool in the summer. Only one of the answers is true. Can you guess the right answer for each animal?

The answers are on page 129.

126

1. Rabbits

A. take cold showers.
B. eat lots of lettuce.
C. let outside air cool blood flowing through their ears.

2. Bees

A. drink iced tea.
B. produce less honey.
C. collect water and pour it over their honeycombs.

3. Dogs

A. bark a lot.
B. shed their top coats.
C. pant.

4. Prairie Dogs

A. curl up in underground burrows.

B. stand under large mammals to shade themselves.

C. wear grass hats.

5. Birds

A. open their beaks and flutter their throats.

B. flap their wings wildly.

C. fly above the clouds.

6. Roadrunners

A. go to a spa.

B. sit still.

C. hang out on cactus branches.

7. Ground Squirrels

A. sleep during the day.
B. shade their bodies with their tails.
C. fan themselves with big oak leaves.

8. Pigs

A. eat ice cream.
B. roll around in mud.
C. lose weight.

Think About It

How are the ways animals keep cool the same as ways humans do?

Hot Animal Quiz Answers

1. C
2. C. The water prevents the beeswax from melting.
3. C. Panting makes air flow over the dog's wet mouth and tongue, whisking away moisture and body heat.
4. A. It's cooler underground!
5. A
6. C. Roadrunners hang out on cactus branches when the sand gets too hot to walk on.
7. B
8. B. Rolling around in mud keeps moisture in a pig's skin.

Response Activities

RAINY DAYS Interview people

Ali's neighbors would probably be indoors on a rainy day.
Find out what people like to do indoors on rainy days.

YOU WILL NEED:

white and gray   scissors   markers
construction paper   or crayons

1. Ask three people who are different ages. You can ask
   your family, your neighbors, or your friends.

2. Write down their answers.

3. Cut out large raindrops from the white and gray paper.

4. Write each person's answer on a raindrop.

Tape your raindrops to a "Rainy Day" bulletin board.

draw

play
games

read

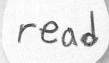

WILD WEATHER Draw a picture

Ali draws pictures of a little lake and an umbrella to make her neighbors feel more comfortable on a hot day. What kind of picture would you draw if it were too hot or too cold outside? What if it were too dark, bright, wet, dry, or windy?

Choose one kind of weather. Then work with a partner to draw a picture that will make everyone feel more comfortable in that kind of weather.

Theme Wrap-Up

Places to Visit...

FOCUS ON SETTINGS ACROSS TEXTS   The setting of a story is when and where the story takes place. Work with a group to make a booklet that tells about the settings in this theme. Tell why each setting is a good place to visit.

1. Draw a picture of each setting.

2. Below each picture, write the story name and a sentence about what you can see there.

3. Make your pictures and sentences into a booklet.

Share the booklet with another group.

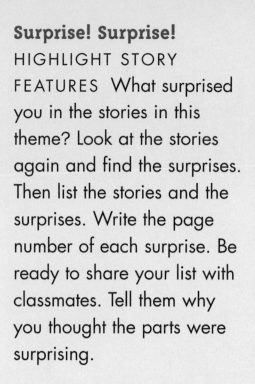

Surprise! Surprise!

HIGHLIGHT STORY FEATURES What surprised you in the stories in this theme? Look at the stories again and find the surprises. Then list the stories and the surprises. Write the page number of each surprise. Be ready to share your list with classmates. Tell them why you thought the parts were surprising.

Trading Places

CHARACTER STUDY Choose a main character from two different stories in this theme. Imagine that you can switch the characters. Now each main character is in the other's story. Write about what you think each character will do in the other's place. Share your writing with your classmates.

THEME
Neighborhood News

CONTENTS

134

Reader's Choice

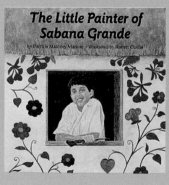

The Little Painter of Sabana Grande

by Patricia Maloney Markun

REALISTIC FICTION

A young artist in Panama has no paper, so he finds something else to paint on.

Notable Trade Book in Social Studies

READER'S CHOICE LIBRARY

The Leaving Morning

by Angela Johnson

REALISTIC FICTION

A family moving to a new home says good-bye to relatives and neighbors.

Award-Winning Author

READER'S CHOICE LIBRARY

Six-Dinner Sid

by Inga Moore

REALISTIC FICTION

Sid the cat pretends to be the pet of six different owners to get six dinners every night.

Notable Trade Book for the Language Arts

Gila Monsters Meet You at the Airport

by Marjorie Weinman Sharmat

REALISTIC FICTION

A boy from New York City is moving to the West, and he's worried about what he may find there.

Award-Winning Author

On an Island in the Bay

by Patricia Mills

NONFICTION

Discover the sights and sounds of life on an island in the Chesapeake Bay.

Parents' Choice

THE

by Fumiko Takeshita

illustrated by Mamoru Suzuki

translated by Ruth A. Kanagy

PARK BENCH

The day has just begun.
A white mist hangs over the park.
No one is here yet, and the park is very still.
Under a tree sits a single white park bench.

The early risers are the first to arrive.
Some do exercises. Others walk their dogs.
The white bench is just now waking up.
Look, here comes the park worker in his
little motor cart.

"Good morning, my dear park bench," says the worker. "It's cleaning day for the park," and he gives the bench a friendly little pat.

Children pass by on their way to school. Adults pass by on their way to work. The town is becoming lively.

Here comes an old man taking his walk. He moves very slowly, leaning on his cane. He stops to smell the flowers and then to feed the birds. He's not in any hurry.

"Now it's time for a rest," says the old man. He sits on the white bench. "The perfect bench in just the right place," he thinks.

Along comes a mother and her baby.
"Let's sit in the sun," she says.
"The white bench is bathed in sunlight."

"Da, da," the baby babbles.
"Goo, goo," the old man replies.
What *can* they be talking about?

Friends meet at the park.
The two mothers begin to chat.
They talk on and on.
Chitter-chatter, chitter-chatter,
until it's time to eat.

All the while
the white bench
listens quietly.

It's lunch time.

The park worker eats under a large tree.

Here come the cats and the birds.

"Okay, my little friends. I'll give you some food,"

he says. "But, oops, don't make the bench dirty."

During the noon hour, lots of people
come to the park to relax.
"This park bench is my favorite spot for a
nap," says a man. A gentle breeze is blowing,
and the park bench begins to feel drowsy, too.

147

A young man waits for his friend who is late.
"Let's meet in the park, at the white bench,"
they had agreed. "But now, where can she be?"

("Wait, who left a book on the bench?" the park
worker wonders.)

Here comes a group of children running to the park.
This is the liveliest time of day.
"What are we going to play today?" asks one child.
"Let's talk it over."

All of a sudden the white bench becomes a house.
Now it's a castle, then an island, now a boat.
Now a train. Then a station. And then, it's even a
park bench again!

Plip plop, plip plop . . .

"Uh-oh, here it comes," says the worker to himself.

Suddenly, it begins to rain.

Everyone runs for shelter.

Everyone except, of course, the white bench.

The rain has stopped.

Now the sky is bright.

The wet flowers and grass glisten.

"You're soaking wet," says the park worker

to the bench, as he gently wipes it dry.

"You're a fine bench in spite of your age," he says.

"I know you'll last for a long, long time."

Now the day is ending. The air becomes chilly.
Children wave to each other as they leave for home.
The white park bench is perfectly still in the twilight.

When the lights go on in the town,
the worker's day is done.
"Good night, my dear white bench," he says.
"You must be very tired. I'll see you tomorrow."
He turns on the lights of his little motor cart
and drives home.

The park is covered with darkness.
Stars twinkle in the sky.
No one is here now, and the park is very still.
Under a tree sits a single white park bench.

Good night.

Think About It

1. How is the park bench special to different people in the community?

2. Would you like to play in a park like this one? Why or why not?

3. Why do you think the author wrote about a park bench?

Meet the Author
and the Illustrator
Fumiko Takeshita

Fumiko Takeshita is a Japanese author. She has written several children's books such as *The Straw Hat*. She has worked with Mamoru Suzuki on another book called *Will Chip Stay at Home?*

Mamoru Suzuki

Mamoru Suzuki is a well-known children's book illustrator in Japan. He went to an art school in Tokyo, the capital city, to learn about illustrating books. In his illustrations, Mamoru Suzuki likes to show what life is like in Japan.

RESPONSE ACTIVITIES

A PARK CARE SIGN

Make a poster

Work with a partner to make a sign that tells people how to take care of a park.

1. Make a list of tips for taking care of a park. Look back at the pictures in the story for ideas.

2. Plan your sign. Think of ways to make it fun to read.

3. Write your tips on your sign. Draw pictures about your tips.

Share your park care sign with classmates.

1. Remember to pick up your trash and throw it away.

2. Take home all the toys you bring to the park.

FUN AT THE PARK Make a collage

Make a collage to show things you like to do at a park. Cut out pictures from old magazines. Glue them on a big sheet of paper.

Below your collage, write sentences that tell what is going on.

Share your collage with classmates.

TIME
The present.

SETTING
Pine Park, a typical town park.

CHARACTERS
Narrator

Lan

Jeff

Mayor Pitt

Police Chief Wilson

Coach Lee

Miss Rosa

156

THE PINE PARK MYSTERY

by Tracey West

illustrated by Mary GrandPré

Award-Winning
Illustrator

SCENE ONE

Narrator: It is a beautiful afternoon in Pine Park. The sun is shining, and the birds are singing. It's just another ordinary day... or is it?

(*Coach Lee, blowing his whistle, runs toward Mayor Pitt.*)

Mayor Pitt: Hello, Coach Lee. It's a great day for a walk in the park, isn't it?

Coach Lee: (*jogging in place*) It sure is, Mayor. Well, I've got to catch up with the team!

(*Coach Lee runs off.*)

Mayor Pitt: Coach Lee is always in a hurry!

(*She sits on a bench and removes her jacket.*)

Mayor Pitt: (*looking at her jacket, confused*) That's funny. I thought I wore my silver pin today. I wonder where it could be!

Narrator: In another part of the park, Lan and Jeff are playing catch.

Lan: I'm bored. Nothing exciting ever seems to happen around here.

(**Jeff** *tosses the ball to* **Lan**.)

Jeff: You're always bored. Isn't playing catch in the park enough fun for you?

(**Lan** *catches the ball and then drops it suddenly, looking confused. She looks closely at her wrist.*)

Lan: That's funny. My charm bracelet is missing. The clasp was loose. . . .

Jeff: Maybe it fell off near here. Let's look.

Narrator: Meanwhile, under a shady tree, Police Chief Wilson is waking up from a nap.

Chief Wilson: There's nothing like taking a nap in the park after working all night on a tough case. Now it's time to get back to the station. A police chief's work is never done.

(**Chief Wilson** *pats his shirt pocket.*)

Chief Wilson: *(confused)* That's funny. My badge is gone! It must be around here somewhere.

Narrator: While Chief Wilson looks for his badge, Coach Lee runs into Miss Rosa. She owns the bookstore downtown.

Miss Rosa: Hi, Coach. Where are you running to?

Coach Lee: I'm trying to find my whistle. I had it a few minutes ago, but now I can't find it anywhere.

Miss Rosa: That's funny—I'm looking for something, too.

Narrator: Is something mysterious happening in Pine Park? Lan and Jeff are about to find out.

161

Missin

Police E

I silver

I whist

SCENE TWO

Narrator: Lan and Jeff see Chief Wilson posting a sign on a tree.

Jeff: *(reading)* Missing: One police badge, one silver pin, and one whistle.

Lan: You can add one charm bracelet to that list, Chief.

Chief Wilson: *(scratching his head)* It's the strangest thing. I can't figure out why all these objects are missing. It's a real mystery.

Lan: A mystery! Now *that* sounds exciting.

SCENE THREE

Narrator: Lan and Jeff are about to try to solve the case of the missing objects.

Lan: We have to think like real detectives, Jeff. Let's start by listing what we know about this case.

Jeff: Well, everyone noticed the objects were missing while they were in the park.

Lan: That's right. What else do we know?

Jeff: All of the objects were pretty small . . . they were all shiny, too.

Lan: I have an idea! Let's put another small, shiny object in the park. Then we can hide and see what happens to it.

Jeff: How about the key to my bicycle lock?

(*Jeff* takes the key from his pocket and puts it on a nearby rock. *Jeff* and *Lan* hide behind a tree. A group of kids runs across the stage, blocking the audience's view of the key on the rock.)

Narrator: There goes Coach Lee's team. But look! The key is gone!

165

SCENE FOUR

(Lan leads Chief Wilson, Mayor Pitt, Coach Lee, and Miss Rosa to a tree in the park, where Jeff is waiting for them.)

Lan: *(to Jeff)* Do you have the thief cornered?

Jeff: *(smiling)* She's up in that tree.

Coach Lee: *(jogging in place)* Thief? I don't see anybody in that tree.

Chief Wilson: *(peers into the tree and smiles)* The thief isn't any*body*, Coach. It's a bird!

Miss Rosa: *(gasps)* That's Dynah! She's my new pet mynah bird. She escaped from the bookstore this morning. I've been looking for her all day! *(looks at **Lan** and **Jeff**)* How did you two know Dynah was the thief?

167

Lan: Jeff figured out that all the missing objects were small and shiny, so we decided to set a trap. We put Jeff's bicycle key on a rock. Dynah flew by and picked it up.

Jeff: Then she flew into this tree.

Miss Rosa: Mynah birds do like to collect shiny objects. I'll bet you'll find all the missing things somewhere in the tree.

Narrator: Chief Wilson calls the Pine Park Fire Department. The firefighters use a ladder to get the objects and bring them down.

Chief Wilson: Here they are—one badge, one silver pin, one whistle, one charm bracelet, and one bicycle key.

169

Miss Rosa: *(holding a bird cage with Dynah in it)* I'm sorry Dynah caused so much trouble, Mayor Pitt. I'll try to keep a close eye on her from now on.

Mayor Pitt: *(laughing)* She certainly caused quite a stir! A day in Pine Park was never so exciting.

Lan: I can't wait to come back to the park tomorrow!

Jeff: To play catch?

Lan: No, I want to see if there's another mystery we can solve!

THINK ABOUT IT

❶ What is the mystery in Pine Park?

❷ What part of the play did you like best?

❸ How do the author and the illustrator give you clues to solve the mystery?

Visit *The Learning Site!*
www.harcourtschool.com

MEET THE AUTHOR

Tracey West loved reading so much as a child that she decided she wanted to be an author. She writes at her home near New York City, where she lives with her husband, her dog, Tisha, and her cat, Elvira.

MEET THE ILLUSTRATOR

Mary GrandPre' has illustrated five children's books and made artwork for an animated film. She lives in St. Paul, Minnesota.

171

Birds Do It! Recycle!

If you collect paper, cloth, string or paper clips, your friends might call you a pack rat. But if you're a bird, you're just building the coolest house in the neighborhood!

You can make a collection box of stuff to leave for birds so they can help themselves. Hang a small plastic box with holes (like the ones berries come in) on a tree branch. Stuff the box loosely with nest-building goodies. Hang the box on a tree and watch birds climb on board to pick through the junk to find their treasures.

Look and see how your old junk can help decorate and warm a bird's new home.

Worn-out shoelaces work well to keep a nest snug and warm.

Bits of cotton help keep a nest warm and cozy.

Birds like yarn. Make sure the strings are no longer than six inches. Otherwise, birds may get tangled up in them and get hurt.

Rags are great. Try to give birds strips of cloth made of natural fibers.

Think About It

What things can you do in your community to help nature?

RESPONSE ACTIVITIES

A TINY PINE PARK PLAY Create a puppet show

Work with a partner to build a shoe-box stage for a scene that you will act out from "The Pine Park Mystery."

You will need:

shoe box • colored paper • glue • scissors • crayons

1. Choose a scene and plan your stage.

2. Glue colored paper inside the shoe box for the background.

3. Draw pictures of characters and objects in the play. Cut out the pictures and glue them onto the shoe-box lid, and cut them out again to make them sturdy.

4. Move the characters around your stage to act out the scene for classmates.

WHAT'S NEXT Add to the story

What mystery will Lan and Jeff solve next?
Write an idea for another mystery that takes
place in Pine Park. Add some new characters.
Share your idea with your classmates.
Can they solve the case before Lan
and Jeff do?

FIRST CLASS

Good-bye,
Curtis

BY KEVIN HENKES
PICTURES BY MARISABINA RUSSO

Award-Winning
Author

PARIS BX ARTS(ε76)
18 H
93
1995
R DES ST PERES (175)

Good-bye,

by Kevin Henkes
pictures by Marisabina Russo

Curtis has been a letter carrier

for forty-two years.

Today is his last day.

Everyone loves Curtis —

the old woman on the hill,

the baby in 4-C,

the clerk at the butcher shop,

and the crossing guard

at the corner of First and Park.

All of the mailboxes all over his route are filled

with all kinds of surprises. There is a chocolate

cupcake with sprinkles from Mrs. Martin.

There is a drawing from Debbie,

Dennis, and Donny.

There is a bottle of aftershave from

the Johnsons, and a box of nuts

from their dog.

There are cards

and candy and cookies.

 There are hugs and

handshakes and kisses.

There is a small, fat book from

Mr. Porter, and a pencil sharpener

in the shape of a mailbox from Max.

"We'll miss you, Curtis,"

say the old woman on the hill

and the baby in 4-C

and the clerk at the butcher shop

and the crossing guard

at the corner of First and Park.

The children Curtis met when

he first began his route have

grown up.

Some of them have children of their own.

Some of them have grandchildren.

Some of the children have had

dogs. Some of the dogs have had puppies.

Cats have had kittens, too.

Trees have grown from little to big.

Houses have been torn down. And houses have

gone up. People have moved out.

And people have moved in.

But everyone loves Curtis.
"We'll miss you," they all say.
The dogs and cats say so, too.

When Curtis gets to the last mailbox
at the last house on the last street . . .

Surprise! Surprise! Surprise!

Curtis's own family is waiting there.
Friends pour out the door and down the steps.
People from all over his route run out from
the backyard.

They have a party in Curtis's honor.
"We love you, Curtis," they all say.
"We'll miss you."

There is dancing and eating and
remembering. There are balloons and
streamers and tiny tin horns.

That night Curtis dreams of his party.
When he wakes up the next morning,
he begins writing thank-you notes to everyone.

And he knows all the addresses by heart.

Think About It

1 What changes did Curtis see during his forty-two years as a letter carrier?

2 Would you like to live along Curtis's route? Why or why not?

3 How do the author and illustrator show that the people on Curtis's route care about him?

Kevin Henkes

Dear Readers,

When I was your age, I loved to go to the library. I carried all my books home by myself, no matter how many I had. I think my visits to the library helped me decide to become an author.

I like to end my stories in a hopeful way. Reading a story with a hopeful ending is like coming home from school and putting on play clothes. It feels good!

Kevin Henkes

Meet the Illustrator
Marisabina Russo

Dear Readers,

When I was a child, I drew pictures all the time. Once I got into trouble for drawing on the bottom of a table. After that my mother gave me a new pad of paper every week. Some of my illustrations in "Good-bye, Curtis" show children and a dog. Can you find them?

Marisabi Russo

Visit *The Learning Site!*
www.harcourtschool.com

Response Activities

Surprise Party! Create an invitation

Imagine that you are having the surprise party for Curtis in your classroom.

On a sheet of paper, make an invitation for your guests. Remember to include this important information:

- For? Surprise party for Curtis

- What day?

- What time?

- Where?

Decorate your invitation and share it with classmates.

Surprise party
For Curtis
On Tuesday
At 1:00
In our classroom

Street Painting Paint a mural

Pretend that you are invited to Curtis's party. With a group, make a painting of a street on Curtis's route as a gift for him.

1. Work together to plan what shops and houses you will paint.

2. Paint your street. Use the pictures in "Good-bye, Curtis" for ideas.

3. Make a sign for each shop. Put a number on each building.

4. Choose a name for your street.

In "Good-bye, Curtis," you read about Curtis's job, his last day at work, and many other things. How will you remember the most important events? A **summary** can help you remember and retell what happens in a story.

A summary tells what a story is mostly about and gives the most important events. It is shorter than the story, and it follows the story's order.

The sentences in this chart tell about story events in "Good-bye, Curtis." Which events would you put in a summary?

Events that are most important	Events that are not as important
• Today is Curtis's last day as a letter carrier.	• Curtis has been a letter carrier for forty-two years.
• The people on his route will miss him.	• Mrs. Martin gives Curtis a chocolate cupcake.
• Curtis's friends and family have a surprise party for him.	• There are tiny tin horns at the party.

In a summary, tell only what the story is mostly about and give only the most important events.

You can summarize a story as you read. This helps you to remember the events better.

WHAT HAVE YOU LEARNED?

1. List the most important story events in "Good-bye, Curtis."

2. In a sentence or two, tell what "Good-bye, Curtis" is mostly about.

TRY THIS • TRY THIS • TRY THIS

Look back at another story that you have read. Think about the most important story events. Summarize the story by writing one sentence about each event.

Visit *The Learning Site!*
www.harcourtschool.com

Award-Winning
Author/Illustrator

198

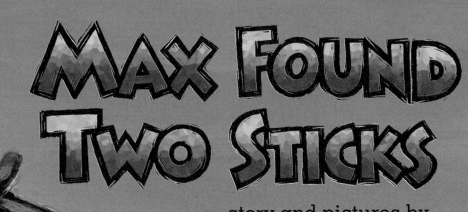

Max Found Two Sticks

story and pictures by

Brian Pinkney

It was a day when Max didn't feel like talking to anyone. He just sat on his front steps and watched the clouds gather in the sky.

A strong breeze shook the tree in front of his house, and Max saw two heavy twigs fall to the ground.

"What are you gonna do with those sticks?" Max's grandpa asked as he washed the front windows.

Not saying a word, Max tapped
on his thighs, *Pat . . . pat-tat.
Putter-putter . . . pat-tat.* His rhythm
imitated the sound of the pigeons,
startled into flight.

When Max's mother came home
carrying new hats for his twin
sisters, she asked, "What are you
doing with Grandpa's cleaning
bucket, Son?"

Max responded by patting the
bucket, *Tap-tap-tap.*

Tippy-tip . . . tat-tat. He created the rhythm of the light rain falling against the front windows.

After a while the clouds moved on and the sun appeared. Cindy, Shaun and Jamal showed up drinking sodas. "Hey, Max! Whatcha doin' with those hatboxes?"

Again Max didn't answer. He just played on the boxes, *Dum . . . dum-de-dum.*

Di-di-di-di. Dum-dum. Max drummed the beat of the tom-toms in a marching band.

"What are you up to with those soda bottles?" his dad asked as he brought out the garbage cans on his way to work.

Max answered on the bottles, *Dong . . . dang . . . dung.*

Ding . . . dong . . . ding!
His music joined the chiming of the bells in the church around the corner.

Soon the twins came out to show off their new hats. "Hey, Max," they asked, "what are you doin' with those garbage cans?"

Max hammered out a reply on the cans, Cling . . . clang . . . da-BANG!

A-cling-clang . . . DA-BANGGGG! Max pounded out the sound of the wheels thundering down the tracks under the train on which his father worked as a conductor.

Suddenly Max heard *Thump-di-di-thump . . . THUMP-DI-DI-THUMP!* as a marching band rounded the corner.

Max watched the drummers with amazement as they passed, copying their rhythms. The last drummer saw Max. Then with a nod and a wink, he tossed Max his spare set of sticks.

"Thanks," called Max—and he didn't miss a beat.

Think About It

1. What kinds of things does Max use to make music?

2. What is your favorite part of the story? Why?

3. How does Max feel at the beginning of the story? How does he feel at the end?

Meet the Author and Illustrator

BRIAN PINKNEY

What made you decide to write this book?

I wanted to write a book about drumming because I've played the drums most of my life. I almost made music my career. I had ideas about a book, but I didn't really have a story. I would jot down notes about a boy and how he liked to drum. It took me about four years to finish the book. I decided to start with the pictures. I would draw a little and then write a little. Most of the words came to me when I was just waking up in the morning or when I was away from my studio.

Visit *The Learning Site!*
www.harcourtschool.com

RESPONSE ACTIVITIES

What will Max do next? Extend the story

Max makes music when he finds two sticks. What will Max do with the next two things he finds?

Choose two things from your classroom that Max might find next. Write a story to tell what Max does with these two things.

Share your story with your classmates.

Making Music

Experiment with rhythm

Max makes music by using only two sticks. What kind of music can you make without using instruments?

Work with a partner. Pick a favorite song. Use your hands and feet to make a tapping, clapping, and snapping rhythm to go with your song.

Share your rhythm song.

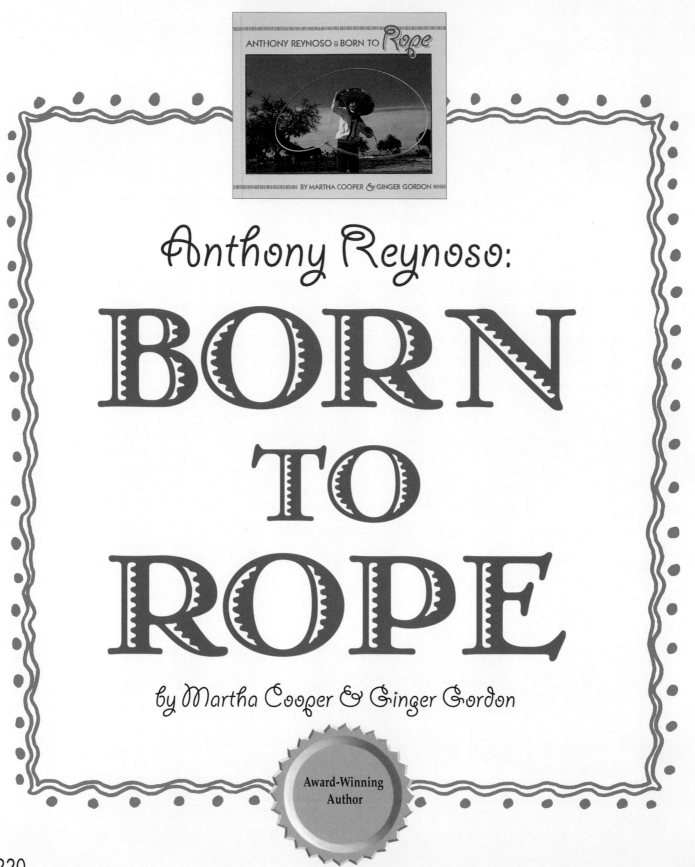

Anthony Reynoso:

BORN TO ROPE

by Martha Cooper & Ginger Gordon

Award-Winning
Author

My name is Anthony Reynoso. I'm named after
my father, who is holding the white horse, and my
grandfather, who is holding the dappled horse.
We all rope and ride Mexican Rodeo style on my
grandfather's ranch outside of Phoenix, Arizona.

As soon as I could stand, my dad gave me a rope. I had my own little hat and everything else I needed to dress as a *charro*. That's what a Mexican cowboy is called. It's a good thing I started when I was little, because it takes years to learn to rope.

I live with my mom and dad in the little
Mexican-American and Yaqui Indian town of
Guadalupe. All my grandparents live close by.
This will help a lot when the new baby comes.
My mom is pregnant.

I've got a secret about Guadalupe. I know where there are petroglyphs in the rocks right near my house. My favorite looks like a man with a shield. People carved these petroglyphs hundreds of years ago. Why did they do it? I wonder what the carvings mean.

Every Sunday morning the old Mexican Mission church is packed. At Easter, lots of people come to watch the Yaqui Indian ceremonies in the center of town.

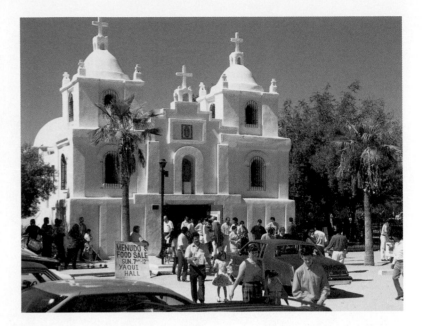

Some Sundays, we go to Casa Reynoso, my grandparents' restaurant. If it's very busy, my cousins and I pitch in. When there's time, my grandmother lets me help in the kitchen. Casa Reynoso has the best Mexican food in town.

On holidays, we go to my grandfather's ranch. Once a year, we all get dressed up for a family photo.

I've got lots of cousins. Whenever there's a birthday we have a piñata. We smash it with a stick until all the candy falls out. Then we scramble to grab as much as we can hold.

Best of all, at the ranch we get to practice roping on horseback. My dad's always trying something new . . . and so am I!

In Mexico, the Rodeo is the national sport. The most famous charros there are like sports stars here.

On weekdays, Dad runs his landscape business,
Mom works in a public school, and I go to school.
I wait for the bus with other kids at the corner
of my block.

I always come to school with
my homework done. When I'm
in class, I forget about roping
and riding. I don't think anyone
in school knows about it except
my best friends.

It's different when I get home. I practice hard with Dad. He's a good teacher and shows me everything his father taught him. We spend a lot of time practicing for shows at schools, malls, and rodeos. We are experts at passing the rope. Our next big exhibition is in Sedona, about two hours away by car.

After rope practice we shoot a few baskets. Dad's pretty good at that too!

On Friday after school, Dad and I prepare our ropes for the show in Sedona. They've got to be just right.

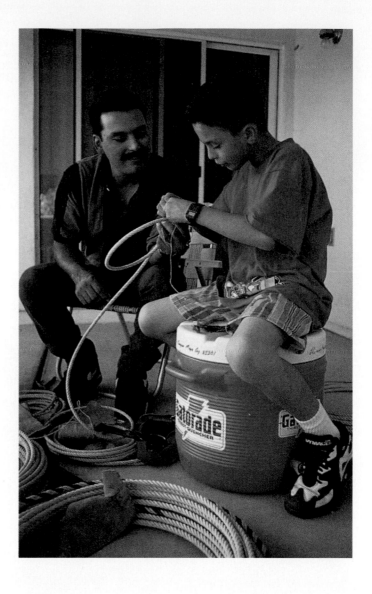

Everything's ready for tomorrow, so I can take a break and go through my basketball cards. I decide which ones I want to buy, sell, and trade. Collecting basketball cards is one of my favorite hobbies.

230

It's Saturday! Time for the show in Sedona. I get a little nervous watching the other performers. I sure wouldn't want to get messed up in my own rope in front of all these people! After the Mexican hat dance, we're next!

My dad goes first . . . and then it's my turn. While the mariachis play, I do my stuff. Even Dad can't spin the rope from his teeth like this!

Then Dad and I rope together, just like we practiced. It's hard to do with our wide charro hats on. When my dad passes the rope to me and I spin it well, he says he has passed the Mexican Rodeo tradition on to me. Now it's up to me to keep it going.

Mom is our best fan. She always comes with us. It makes me feel good to know she's out there watching.

Sometimes tourists want us to pose for pictures with them. It makes me feel like a celebrity.

After the show, boy, are we hungry! We pack up and eat a quick lunch. Then we go to a special place called Slide Rock. Slide Rock is a natural water slide where kids have played for hundreds, maybe even thousands, of years. It's cold today! I'd rather come back in the summer when it's hot. But Dad pulls me in anyway. Brrr!

Time to go home. Next time we come to Sedona, the baby will be with us. I wonder if it will be a boy or a girl. It's hard to wait! I'm going to love being a big brother. Pretty soon the baby will be wearing my old boots and learning how to rope from me.

THINK ABOUT IT

1. What does Anthony tell you about his life?

2. What kind of skill would you like to learn? Why?

3. Why is Mexican Rodeo tradition important to the Reynoso family?

Ginger Gordon is a first-grade teacher and a writer. She has written another book with Martha Cooper called *My Two Worlds*. The book is about an 8-year-old girl who lives in both New York City and the Dominican Republic. Ginger Gordon likes to show what life is like for children in different cultures.

Martha Cooper is a photographer. She likes to show how people from many different backgrounds live together in neighborhoods. Her photographs can be found in magazines, books, calendars, and museum shows. Martha Cooper lives in New York City.

Visit *The Learning Site!* www.harcourtschool.com

RESPONSE

MY STORY Write a personal story

Anthony Reynoso likes to rope and collect trading
cards. Write a story about what you like to do.
Use the word *I* to tell your story the way
Anthony Reynoso does. Give your story a title.

Add your story to a class book.
Put the book in the reading center.

ACTIVITIES

FAMILY FUN ALBUM

Add to a picture album

Anthony Reynoso likes to do many things with his family. Work with a group. Draw a picture of something that Anthony likes to do with his family. Look back at the story for ideas.

Share your picture with your group. Then add your picture to your group members' pictures. Put them all together in a Family Fun Album.

Main Idea

"**A**nthony Reynoso: Born to Rope" tells about a boy who is learning to be a charro. This is the **topic** of the story. The rest of the story gives information about the topic.

Most paragraphs in a story have a **main idea** and **important details**. The main idea is what the paragraph is mostly about. Important details are pieces of information that tell more about the main idea. Finding the main ideas can help you organize the story ideas.

Reread this paragraph from the story:

Some Sundays, we go to Casa Reynoso, my grandparents' restaurant. If it's very busy, my cousins and I pitch in. When there's time, my grandmother lets me help in the kitchen. Casa Reynoso has the best Mexican food in town.

The sentence in the box tells the main idea of the paragraph. The other sentences are important details.

As you read a story, think about the main idea in each paragraph. The main ideas can help you figure out the important information.

WHAT HAVE YOU LEARNED?

Reread the second paragraph on page 230 of "Anthony Reynoso: Born to Rope."

1 What is the main idea of the paragraph?

2 What are the important details?

TRY THIS • TRY THIS • TRY THIS

Look back at a paragraph from another story that you have read. Find the main idea. Tell a partner about the paragraph and its main idea.

 Visit *The Learning Site!*
www.harcourtschool.com

Theme Wrap-Up

Let's Search!

REVIEW THE LITERATURE
Think about the stories in this theme, and decide on your favorite. Then search through that story to find the section that was the most interesting to you. Tell your classmates why you think it is the most interesting.

A Perfect Fit

THEME CONNECTIONS Choose a story from Neighborhood News.
Then ask yourself why this story belongs in this theme. Compare your
answer with those of classmates who chose the same story you did.

Character Chat!

CONDUCT AN INTERVIEW
Work with a group to host a
TV talk show. The characters in
this theme will be your guests.
Decide who will take the part
of each character and who will
be the host. Work together to
write a few questions for the host
to ask. For example, the host
might ask about each character's
home and community. Group
members playing the guests
should answer the way their story
characters would. Invite
your classmates to be the
audience for your talk show.

THEME

TRAVEL TIME

CONTENTS

Grandpa Takes Me to the Moon
by Timothy R. Gaffney

FANTASY

A boy imagines that he travels with his grandfather to the moon.

READER'S CHOICE LIBRARY

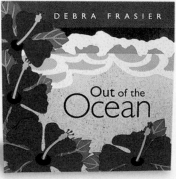

Out of the Ocean
by Debra Frasier

REALISTIC FICTION

A young girl and her mother discover sea treasures.

Award-Winning Author
READER'S CHOICE LIBRARY

The Sun and Other Stars
by Richard Harris

NONFICTION

Learn about our sun, other stars, and some mysteries of the universe.

Where Does the Trail Lead?
by Burton Albert

REALISTIC FICTION

A young boy finds adventure on an island.

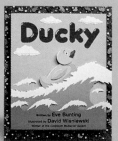

Ducky
by Eve Bunting

FICTION

A yellow plastic duck makes a long journey when he is washed overboard in a storm.

Award-Winning Author
Award-Winning Illustrator

Montigue on the High Seas

story and pictures by
John Himmelman

Award-Winning
Author

 In a cozy hole by the sea, there lived a young mole. His name was Montigue. Montigue loved his home. It was cool in the afternoons and warm in the evenings.

One day it began to rain. Soon the rain was coming down in buckets. By evening, Montigue's home was flooded. He had to find a safe place to spend the night. Montigue swam and swam until at last he noticed a funny-looking house propped on a rock. He was so tired that he fell into a deep sleep as soon as he crawled inside.

Montigue woke up rested and warm. It was a few moments before he realized that he had been . . .

 . . . swept out to sea!

Poor Montigue drifted for days with nothing to drink except lime soda and nothing to eat but seaweed.

He grew lonely and bored as he stared at the horizon day after day. Then one morning, he noticed a dark shadow beneath him. Suddenly, he was thrown into the air by a giant humpback whale! Montigue clung to the bottle as it slowly filled with water and sank.

251

A passing fish, spotting an interesting
meal, swallowed the bottle, mole
and all! Before Montigue knew what
was happening, the fish was yanked
up by a huge net. Montigue and the bottle fell out
of its mouth and onto the deck of a ship.

Montigue looked up half-dazed and saw a giant
sailor looming over him. He was holding a giant
cat! The cat leapt after him, but Montigue

scuttled into a hole.
"Safe at last," he thought.

"What a funny-looking
mouse," said a voice
beside him.

Montigue was surrounded by mice. "What were you doing out there?" asked one, nervously. "Don't you know that Barnacles the Cat is trying to clear us all off this ship?"

Montigue began to tell them how he came to the ship. He told of battling raging seas, riding giant whales, fighting off mole-eating fish, and he told them of the crash of his bottle ship. Just as he was coming to the end of his story, Montigue fell off his perch and knocked over a box of kitchen supplies.

When things settled down, the mice cheered. Montigue had given them an idea. The mice scurried in every direction, collecting bits of cloth, rags, and other supplies. Even Montigue got caught up in the fun.

They all worked together and soon their fleet was launched. The mice elected Montigue their captain. As they glided over the sea, he began to enjoy the thrill of guiding the ships through the waves. In a few days, one of the mice shouted, "LAND HO!"

When they were safely ashore, the mice carried Montigue on their shoulders. They asked him to live with them and he happily accepted. They started building their homes right away.

Montigue loved his new home. It was cool in the afternoons and warm in the evenings. And now he had lots of friendly neighbors.

And if he ever felt the pull of the high seas, he still had his bottle and his sail.

Think About It

1 What happens to Montigue while he is on the high seas?

2 What part of Montigue's adventure do you like the best?

3 Why do you think the author has Montigue meet the mice on the ship?

Meet the Author and Illustrator

John Himmelman

John Himmelman gets the ideas for his stories from the pictures he draws of characters like Montigue. The pictures help him to know what a character will do in a story. "A story is just a story, but the characters become very real to me," he says. When he's not creating children's books, John Himmelman likes to play the guitar.

Visit *The Learning Site!*
www.harcourtschool.com

Response Activities

Montigue Sails Again!

Montigue Sails Again! Add to the story

Write a story about Montigue going on another
adventure in his bottle. Tell what happens
to him on the sea and on land.

Write your story on a bottle-shaped
sheet of construction paper.
Add your story to a class
bulletin board called
"Montigue's Adventures."

Montigue floated
all day. A big
bird picked up
his bottle.

Tell a Tale with Pictures Make a story mural

Work together to retell "Montigue on the High Seas" in pictures.
Paint your pictures on a big sheet of paper.

You will need: mural paper

paintbrushes

paint

1. Plan who will paint each part of
   the story.

2. Paint pictures to tell the story. Use the pictures
   in "Montigue on the High Seas" for ideas.

3. Use the pictures to tell the story aloud.

4. Invite another class to hear your tale.

Cause and Effect

In "Montigue on the High Seas," you learned about Montigue's adventures. Why did each of his adventures happen?

Look at this chart. Read the sentence about the story:

Montigue scuttled into a hole,

because the cat leapt after him.

EFFECT

CAUSE

The first part of the sentence tells you that Montigue scuttled into a hole. This is the **effect**. It tells you what happened because of something else.

The second part of the sentence tells you that the cat leapt after Montigue. This is the **cause**. It tells you why something happened. You know that Montigue scuttled into a hole *because* the cat leapt after him.

As you read, think about what is happening in the story and why these things are happening. Think about why the characters do and say things. Look for words such as *because*, *so*, and *but* that authors might use to connect a cause with an effect.

Why is the cat climbing the tree?

WHAT HAVE YOU LEARNED?

1 Finish this sentence: Montigue left his home because _____.

2 What happened when Montigue's bottle was thrown into the air by a humpback whale?

TRY THIS • TRY THIS • TRY THIS

Look back at another story that you have read. Write about something that happens in the story. Trade papers with a partner. Have your partner write why that thing happens. Then talk about the events.

Visit *The Learning Site!*
www.harcourtschool.com

DINOSAURS

A Guide for Families on the Go

DINOSAURS TRAVEL
A GUIDE FOR FAMILIES ON THE GO
Laurie Krasny Brown and Marc Brown

Award-Winning Author and Illustrator

◆ **Laurie Krasny Brown and Marc Brown**

TRAVEL

Traveling

Do you ever wish you could climb a mountain,

fly through the air,

or ride around town in a long limousine?

HELEN'S HOT DOGS WORLD FAMOUS

KOSHER

Every time you leave home,
whether to travel

around the world,

or around the block,
get ready for an adventure!

267

Getting Ready for a Trip

Books and maps can help you learn about a new place before you go there.

You may not be able to take your pets with you, but someone else will take good care of them.

If you take the addresses of friends and relatives, you can write to them while you're away.

Find out about the weather where you're going and choose clothes that will be good to wear. Only pack a few toys, games, books, and tapes. Small, light, and sturdy things travel best.

Remember one or two favorite companions.

And don't forget these!

Getting From Place to Place

Wherever you're headed, getting there can be part of the fun!

On Foot

Walking lets you stop
and see the sights.

You may meet other travelers
along the way.

You can hike on a trail where
almost no one ever goes.

And your body is all that
you need!

Your Own Wheels

Bicycles and skateboards are faster than walking. You're the driver! It's up to you to know the rules of the road.

Keep your bike or board in good working order, so you're all set to ride anytime.

With your own set of wheels, you can go most anywhere!

You and your family can go biking together.

Sometimes you have to pedal hard to get where you're going,

but downhill you get a free ride!

By Car

Cars will take you on all kinds of roads. Riding on the highways is fastest!

Driving on back roads is slower but you see more.

You and your family can go wherever or whenever you want. You can bring along lots of your things—if you have room!

You and your family can play
word games while you ride. You
can take turns reading road signs
or looking at different license plates.

It feels good to get out and stretch
your legs from time to time.

Switching seats will give you
different views.

If you have a cassette player, you
can bring your favorite tapes.

Riding the Subway and Bus

In some cities riding underground in a subway is the fastest way to travel.

On a bus you can see what's going on outside. A tour bus driver will point out the sights.

On a subway or bus you must pay a fare to ride.

Subways and buses make many stops. Don't forget to watch for yours!

Taking the Train

You can buy a ticket for the train at the station. Look at the signs for your track and departure time. All aboard! Taking the train is a great way to see new places!

On most trains, you can sit facing forward or backward. The conductor announces each stop the train makes. You can follow along with a timetable.

Trains don't have to stop until they pull into a station. The train stops at many stations so passengers can get on and off.

Flying in Planes

At the airport an agent looks at your ticket, checks your luggage, and assigns you a seat on the plane.

Airport security makes sure no one carries anything dangerous or illegal on the plane.

You can bring a small bag on most planes and stow it under or above your seat. Buckle up!

Take off!

As the plane climbs higher, things below look smaller and smaller.

You'll fly up above the clouds!

Coming Home

When it's time to go home, remember to pack all your things. You may want to bring back a gift for someone special. Souvenirs and pictures will remind you of your trip.

At home, things may look different to you.

It's fun to go home again and see friends and relatives.

You can play with all your toys, eat your favorite snacks, and dream about where to travel next!

Think About It

1 What are some important things to remember before and as you travel?

2 Where would you go for an adventure? How would you get there?

3 If the Browns asked you to add a travel tip to this book, what would you write?

Meet the Author

Laurie Krasny Brown

Dear Reader,

I've written a lot of books, but *Dinosaurs Travel* is special to me. You see, I wrote the words, and my husband, Marc Brown, drew the pictures.

Whenever I start to write a book, I read all I can on the subject. Next, I make a list of what I need to put in the book. Then, I write and rewrite. When I am done, I get someone who knows a lot about what's in the book to read it.

Your friend,

Laurie Krasny Brown

Visit *The Learning Site!*
www.harcourtschool.com

Meet the Illustrator

Marc Brown

Dear Reader,

Many kids know my artwork from my Arthur books, but I like to do information books, too. I have done several books using these dinosaur characters. I chose to draw dinosaurs because they are powerful animals, and I want my readers to feel powerful. I am proud of these books because I think they help kids feel good about themselves.

When I am not working, I like to spend time gardening. My wife, Laurie, and I grow flowers, fruits, and vegetables.

Your friend,

Marc Brown

w-h-e-

Wheels on a wagon, Wheels on a bike,

Wheels on my skates, Let me go where I like.

Wheels on a bus, Wheels on a car,

Wheels on a train, Take me so far.

How fast could I go, How far would I get,

If wheels had not been invented yet?

by Florence Parry Heide

RESPONSE ACTIVITIES

A People Mover Invent a travel machine

People travel in all kinds of ways. Now think of a new way to travel. Work with a partner to make a travel machine.

1. Talk about what is special about the machine and where you want it to take you.

2. On a sheet of paper, draw a picture of your machine.

3. Below your picture, write some sentences that tell what your machine can do.

4. Share your machine with your classmates.

Pack Your Suitcase

Make a list

Choose a place you want to visit. It may be the seashore, the desert, the mountains, or the woods. It may be nearby or far away.

Write a list of the things you would need to pack in your suitcase. Draw a picture of the one thing you *must* take.

Share your list and picture with a group. Tell why you packed each thing.

1. toothbrush
2. hiking boots
3. cap
4. sweater
5. backpack

Abuela

Abuela

by Arthur Dorros
illustrated by Elisa Kleven

ALA
Notable Book

Notable Trade Book
in Social Studies

by Arthur Dorros

illustrated by Elisa Kleven

Abuela takes me on the bus. We go all around
the city.

Abuela is my grandma. She is my mother's mother.
Abuela means "grandma" in Spanish.
Abuela speaks mostly Spanish because that's what
people spoke where she grew up, before she came to this
country. Abuela and I are always going places.

Today we're going to the park.
"El parque es lindo," says Abuela.
I know what she means. I think the park is beautiful too.

"Tantos pájaros," Abuela says
as a flock of birds surrounds us.
So many birds. They're picking up the bread we brought.

What if they picked me up
and carried me
high above the park?
What if I could fly?
Abuela would wonder where I was.
Swooping like a bird, I'd call to her.

Then she'd see me flying.
Rosalba the bird.
"Rosalba el pájaro," she'd say.
"Ven, Abuela. Come, Abuela," I'd say.
"Sí, quiero volar," Abuela would reply
as she leaped into the sky
with her skirt flapping in the wind.

We would fly all over the city.
"Mira," Abuela would say, pointing.

And I'd look, as we soared
over parks and streets, dogs and people.

We'd wave to the people waiting for the bus.
"Buenos días," we'd say.
"Buenos días. Good morning,"
they'd call up to us. We'd fly
over factories and trains . . .

292

and glide close to the sea.
"Cerca del mar," we'd say.
We'd almost touch the tops of waves.

Abuela's skirt would be a sail.
She could race with the sailboats.
I'll bet she'd win.

We'd fly to where the ships are docked,
and watch people unload fruits
from the land where Abuela grew up.
Mangos, bananas, papayas—
those are all Spanish words.
So are rodeo, patio, and burro.
Maybe we'd see a cousin of Abuela's
hooking boxes of fruit to a crane.
We saw her cousin Daniel once,
unloading and loading the ships.

Out past the boats in the harbor
we'd see the Statue of Liberty.
"Me gusta," Abuela would say.
Abuela really likes her.
I do too.

We would circle around Liberty's head
and wave to the people visiting her.
That would remind Abuela of when
she first came to this country.

"Vamos al aeropuerto," she'd say.
She'd take me to the airport where
the plane that first brought her landed.
"Cuidado," Abuela would tell me.
We'd have to be careful
as we went for a short ride.

Then we could fly to *tío* Pablo's
and *tía* Elisa's store.
Pablo is my uncle, my *tío*,
and Elisa is my aunt, my *tía*.
They'd be surprised when we flew in,
but they'd offer us a cool *limonada*.
Flying is hot work.
"Pero quiero volar más,"
Abuela would say.
She wants to fly more.
I want to fly more too.

We could fly to *las nubes*, the clouds.
One looks like a cat, *un gato*.
One looks like a bear, *un oso*.
One looks like a chair, *una silla*.
"Descansemos un momento,"
Abuela would say.
She wants to rest a moment.
We would rest in our chair,
and Abuela would hold me in her arms,
with the whole sky
our house, *nuestra casa*.

We'd be as high as airplanes,
balloons, and birds,
and higher than the tall buildings downtown.
But we'd fly there too
to look around.

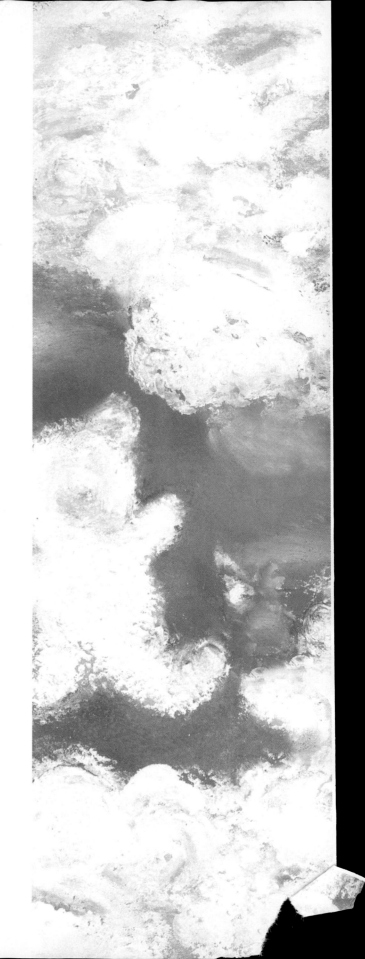

We could find the building where my father works.
"Hola, papá," I'd say as I waved. And Abuela would
do a flip for fun as we passed by the windows.

"Mira," I hear Abuela say.
"Look," she's telling me.
I do look,
and we are back in the park.

We are walking by the lake.
Abuela probably wants to go for a boat ride.
"Vamos a otra aventura," she says.
She wants us to go for another adventure.
That's just one of the things I love
about Abuela.
She likes adventures.

Abuela takes my hand.
"*Vamos,*" she says.
"Let's go."

Think About It

1. What adventures do Rosalba and Abuela have in the city?

2. Would you like to travel with Rosalba and Abuela? Explain your answer.

3. How would this story be different if Rosalba and Abuela were walking instead of flying?

Glossary

The capitalized syllable is stressed in pronunciation.

Abuela (ah-BWEH-lah)   Grandmother

Buenos días (BWEH-nohs DEE-ahs)   Good day

Cerca del mar (SEHR-kah dehl mahr)   Close to the sea

Cuidado (kwee-DAH-doh)   Be careful

Descansemos un momento (dehs-kahn-SEH-mohs oon moh-MEHN-toh)   Let's rest a moment

El parque es lindo (ehl PAHR-kay ehs LEEN-doh)   The park is beautiful

Hola, papá (OH-lah, pah-PAH)   Hello, papa

Las nubes (lahs NOO-behs)   The clouds

Limonada (lee-moh-NAH-dah)   Lemonade

Me gusta (meh GOO-stah)   I like

Mira (MEE-rah)   Look

Nuestra casa (NWEH-strah CAH-sah)   Our house

Pero quiero volar más (PEH-roh key-EH-roh boh-LAR mahs)   But I would like to fly more

Rosalba el pájaro (roh-SAHL-bah ehl PAH-hah-roh)   Rosalba the bird

Sí, quiero volar (see, key-EH-roh boh-LAR)   Yes, I want to fly

Tantos pájaros (TAHN-tohs PAH-hah-rohs)   So many birds

Tía (TEE-ah)   Aunt

Tío (TEE-oh)   Uncle

Un gato (oon GAH-toh)   A cat

Un oso (oon OH-soh)   A bear

Una silla (OON-ah SEE-yah)   A chair

Vamos (BAH-mohs)   Let's go

Vamos al aeropuerto (BAH-mohs ahl ah-ehr-oh-PWEHR-toh)   Let's go to the airport

Vamos a otra aventura (BAH-mohs ah OH-trah ah-behn-TOO-rah)   Let's go on another adventure

Ven (behn)   Come

Meet the Author
Arthur Dorros

Dear Readers,

"Abuela" is about my New York grandmother and about imagining flying. When I was in the second grade, I liked to fly kites. I watched my kite rise until it was just a tiny dot in the sky. I imagined what it would be like to soar in the sky like a bird.

Later, I could see much of New York City from the apartment building I lived in. The city appeared below, as it did for Rosalba and Abuela in the story. Imagine how your home might look from high above!

Your friend,

Arthur Dorros

Meet the Illustrator
Elisa Kleven

Visit *The Learning Site!*
www.harcourtschool.com

Dear Readers,

I enjoyed making the pictures for "Abuela." I did not know New York City very well, so Arthur Dorros drew a map to show me the places where Rosalba and Abuela would fly.

When I made the artwork for this story, I first drew pencil illustrations. Then I used pens, crayons, watercolors, and collage materials to finish the artwork. I even used some material from a blouse of mine to make Abuela's purse!

Your friend,

Elisa Kleven

Response Activities

Come Fly with Me Draw a picture

If Rosalba and Abuela flew over your neighborhood, what would they see?

- Look at the pictures in "Abuela." Everything on the ground looks smaller.

- Plan how you will show your home or school from the air. Draw your picture.

- Write a sentence to tell what the characters are saying.

- Share your picture.

MORE
ADVENTURES

BY ROBBIE AND JAN

Another Adventure Extend the story

On their adventure, Abuela and Rosalba go flying through the air. Now, they are ready for a new adventure, sailing on a boat. Work with a partner. Write what they would see and do. Choose a way to share your new story. You might make a book or record your story on tape.

Word Endings

ou have learned that you can add word endings such as *-s, -ed,* and *-ing* to base words. Another kind of word ending is a suffix. A **suffix** is a word part that adds meaning to a base word.

In "Abuela," Rosalba says this sentence:

We'd have to be careful as we went for a short ride.

What base word do you see in the word *careful*? You see that the letters *ful* have been added to the end of the base word *care*.

The word part *-ful* is a suffix. It adds the meaning "full of." You can see that the word *careful* means "full of care."

Now, read the words in the first column of this chart. Look for the base word and the suffix.

word	=	base word	+	suffix
slowly	=	slow	+	ly
kindness	=	kind	+	ness

The suffix *-ly* makes the base word tell how. The word *slowly* means "in a slow way." The suffix *-ness* adds the meaning of "being" to the base word. The word *kindness* means "being kind."

Look for words that are made up of base words and suffixes. Think about the meanings the suffixes add. This can help you figure out the meaning of longer words.

RUTH LAW

Notable Trade Book in Social Studies

story and pictures by Don Brown

THRILLS A NATION

On November 19, 1916, Ruth Law tried to fly from Chicago to New York City in one day.

It had never been done before.

It was a frosty, blustery morning. Ruth woke up before dawn, but she did not feel the cold. To get used to the cold weather, she had slept in a tent on the roof of a Chicago hotel.

She put on two woolen suits, one on top of the other.

Then she put on two leather suits and covered her bulky outfit with a skirt.

In 1916, a polite lady *always* wore a skirt.

It was still dark when Ruth went to Grant Park on the Lake Michigan shore, where her plane was waiting. It was the tiny one she flew in air shows. Ruth called it a baby machine. It was good for stunts like loop-the-loop, but it was small and old. Ruth had tried to buy a newer, bigger plane for her long flight, but Mr. Curtiss, the manufacturer, had refused to sell her one. Hundreds of pilots had already been injured or killed flying, and Mr. Curtiss did not believe a woman could fly a large plane.

Mechanics had worked all night on the plane. They had attached a special windshield to protect Ruth from the cold wind, and had added a second gas tank so she would not have to stop for fuel more than once. Now the plane could carry fifty-three gallons of gasoline. But the additional gasoline made the plane too heavy. To get rid of some extra weight, the mechanics took the lights off the plane. Without them, Ruth would have to reach New York City before nightfall.

The freezing weather made the engine hard to start. More than an hour passed before Ruth could get under way.

At 7:20 A.M., Ruth climbed into the cockpit. She removed her skirt and stuffed it behind her seat—good sense defeated fashion.

She opened the throttle. The plane leaped forward and bounced over bumps and hollows. It raced awkwardly across the ground, then lifted toward the sky.

A fierce wind whipped through Chicago. It shook and tossed the small plane.

A dozen onlookers watched in fear.

A mechanic cried.

Ruth struggled to steady the plane as it dipped and pitched in the wind.

She narrowly topped the buildings and slowly climbed into the sky above Chicago. Ruth Law was on her way to New York City.

A mile above ground, Ruth sliced through the frigid winter air at one hundred miles an hour. She set her course by consulting the crude scroll of maps she had taped together and attached to her leg. She also had a compass, a clock, and a speedometer.

Ruth flew for nearly six hours. She was depending on the wind to help carry her from Chicago to New York City. But the wind died down. Only gasoline propelled the plane.

At approximately 2:00 P.M. eastern standard time, she neared Hornell, New York, where a group of supporters was waiting.

Then the engine quit.

The fuel tank was empty and Hornell was still two miles away.

The plane pitched slightly and sank. Ruth had only one chance to make a safe landing.

She struggled to control the steering gear. The field seemed to
come up at her. The crowd of spectators spilled into her path.
The plane brushed their heads.

Ruth was on the ground.

She was so cold and hungry that she had to be helped to a nearby car. She was driven to a restaurant for a lunch of scrambled eggs and coffee while her plane was refueled.

She had flown 590 miles nonstop. It was a record. No one in America had ever flown farther.

But Ruth's flight was not over.

At 3:24 P.M., Ruth set out again for New York City.

All day, newspapers told the story of Ruth's flight. A
crowd in Binghamton, New York, had turned out, hoping
to see her fly overhead. They were not disappointed. At
first she was just a speck in the sky, but soon she made a
striking cameo against the late afternoon sun.

Suddenly the plane slanted toward the ground and disappeared behind some trees.

"She's down! Something's broken!"

Nothing was broken. Ruth had decided to land. New York
City was two hours away, but she would not be able to read her
instruments in the dark. She tied the plane to a tree, wrapped
her skirt around her, and accepted the hospitality of strangers.

The next morning, Ruth flew to New York City.

When she landed, an army general and a military band were there to greet her. Ruth was a heroine. "You beat them all!" the general said as he shook her hand.

Newspapers heralded her feat.

President Woodrow Wilson called her great.

A huge banquet was given in her honor.

On November 19, 1916, Ruth Law tried to fly from Chicago to New York City in one day and failed. Still, she set an American nonstop cross-country flying record—590 miles!—and thrilled a nation.

Her record stood for one year. It was broken by Katherine Stinson, another pilot who dared.

THINK ABOUT IT

❶ How did Ruth Law thrill the nation?

❷ What do you think it would have been like to have been a member of Ruth Law's plane crew?

❸ Why do you think the author wanted to tell Ruth Law's story?

 Visit *The Learning Site!* www.harcourtschool.com

Don Brown

Don Brown loves to read and write about history. While
writing a magazine article about flight, he became interested
in the early flyers. He didn't want brave pilots like Ruth Law
to be forgotten. This is his first children's book.

LAST LAUGH

They all laughed when I told them
I wanted to be

A woman in space
Floating so free.

But they won't laugh at me
When they finally see
My feet up on Mars
And my face on TV.

by Lee Bennett Hopkins
illustrated by Nancy Coffelt

Ruth Law
and Katherine
Stinson were
not the only
women to fly...

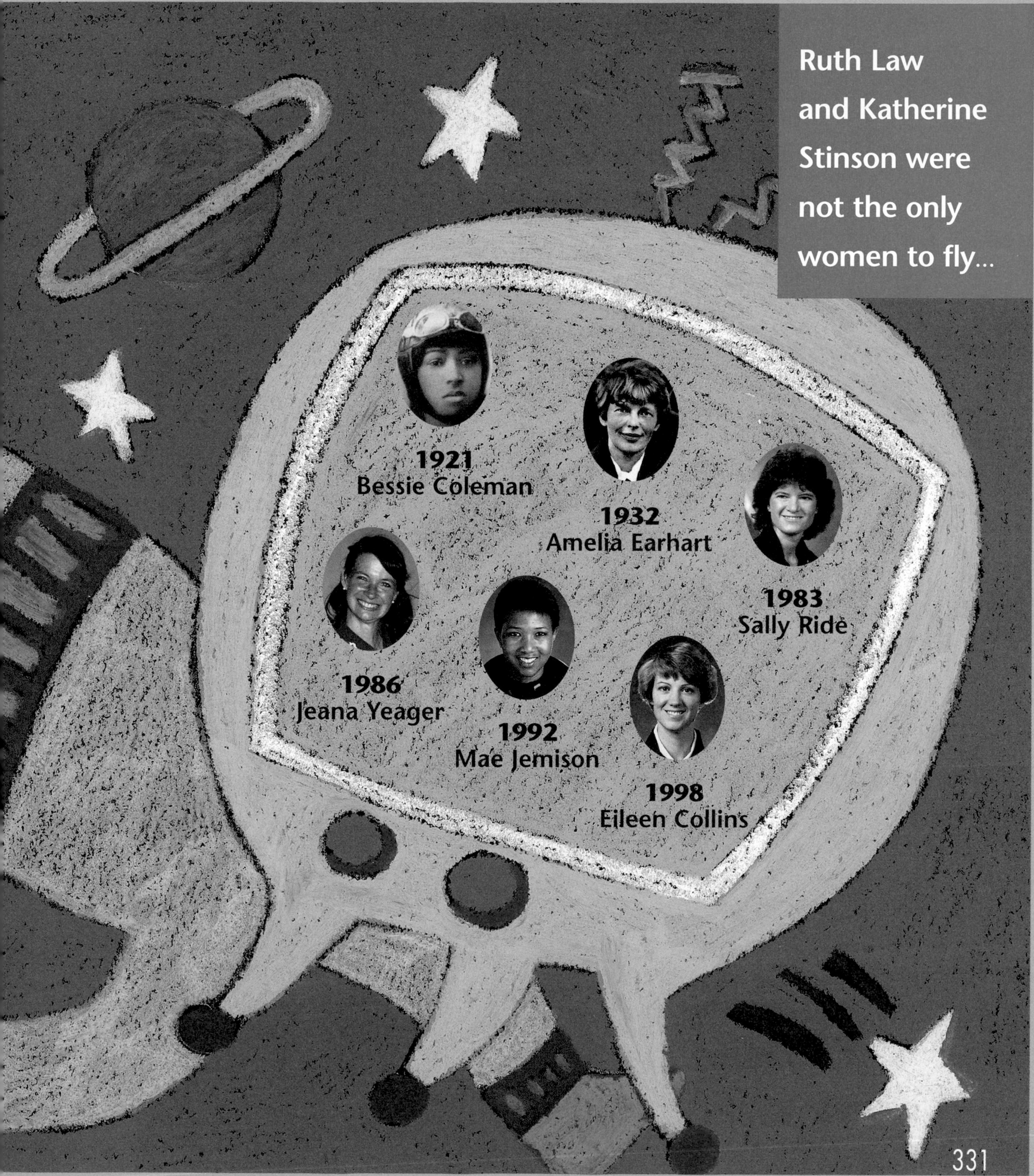

1921
Bessie Coleman

1932
Amelia Earhart

1983
Sally Ride

1986
Jeana Yeager

1992
Mae Jemison

1998
Eileen Collins

READ ALL ABOUT IT   Write a news story

Pretend that you are a newspaper reporter. Write a news story about Ruth Law's flight.

1. Think of what you can ask Ruth before and after her trip. Write a list of questions that begin with *who, what, where, when, how,* and *why.*

2. Write your story. Don't forget to add a headline.

Publish your news story.

Woman Hero Takes Flight

Aviator Ruth Law Flies from Chicago to New York City!

NEW YORK CITY–Today, November 20, 1916, Miss Ruth Law of Chicago flew her biplane into New York City and landed with a military band playing a welcome song. She shook hands with the army general present to witness her landing, and the general remarked, "You beat them all!"

President Woodrow Wilson was not present for the landing because he was needed in Washington D.C. at the White House, but he called Miss Law a heroine, saying she was great. A huge party was given to honor Miss Law's amazing flight and many people came to congratulate her.

Ruth Law wanted to make the trip from Chicago to New York City in one day. She began her flight at 7:20 a.m. from Grant Park in downtown Chicago. She flew at 100 miles an hour! After flying for 590 miles without stopping, she landed in Hornell, New York, to get more gasoline for her plane. While she was there she stopped to have some lunch. At 3:24 p.m. Miss Law got back in her plane and flew toward New York City.

Late in the afternoon, she landed near Binghamton, New York. She ran out of daylight, and she knew she wouldn't be able to read her maps or the instruments in the dark. She stayed at the home of

Ruth Law makes a close landing after running out of gasoline!

While her plane is being refueled, Ruth Law has lunch with the people at a restaurant in Hornell, New York.

Ruth Law attends a special

ADVENTURE IN THE SKY Write a poem

Imagine that you are Ruth Law. How do you feel about flying across the country? Write a poem that Ruth Law might have written after her adventure. Choose a way to share your poem with classmates.

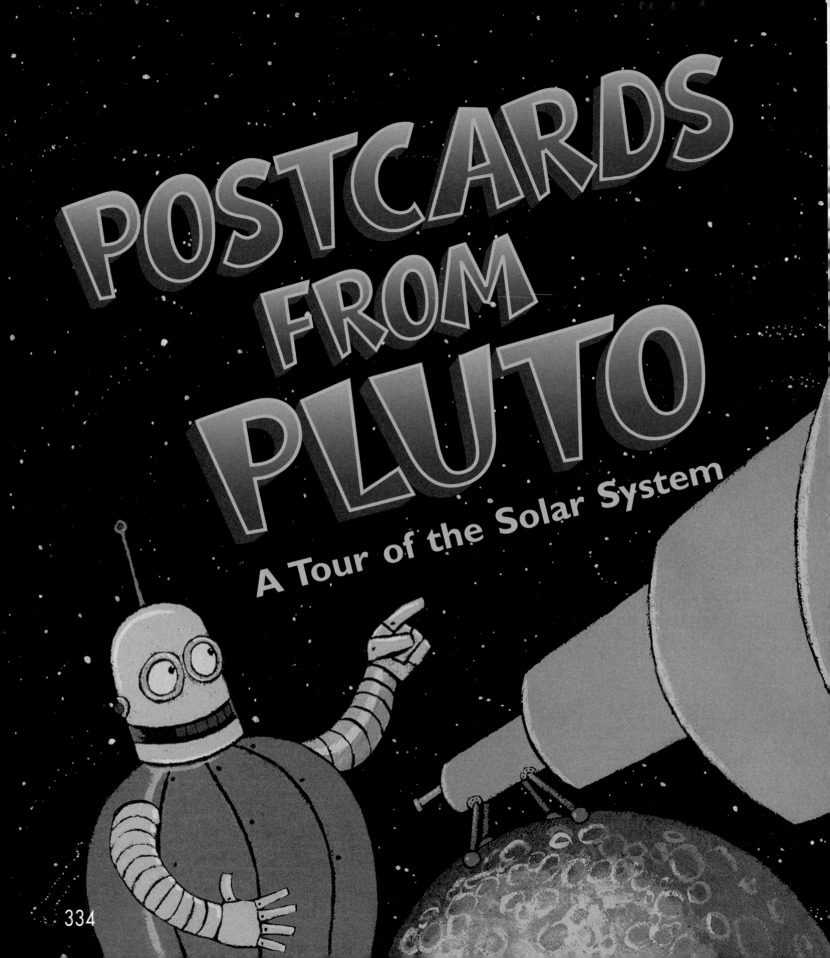

POSTCARDS FROM PLUTO

A Tour of the Solar System

Sun

Mercury

Venus

Earth

asteroid belt

Mars

Welcome aboard! I'm Dr. Quasar, your tour guide. You probably know a lot about space already, and as we travel through the solar system, you'll find out much more.

Take a look at this model. All the planets, moons, asteroids, and comets travel around a star we call the SUN. The ASTEROIDS form a ring around the Sun.

ERIC

MINDA

Heavenly Rocks

orbit

planet

moon

Sun

orbit

planet

planet

Everything in the solar system is in motion. Each planet ROTATES, or spins. The planets ORBIT, or travel around, the Sun. A MOON orbits a planet.

Milky Way galaxy

our solar system

Our solar system is part of a huge group of stars called a GALAXY that is rotating through the universe. We are here—in the Milky Way galaxy.

So we are rotating and orbiting at the same time?

Right.

I'm getting dizzy!

ERIC

The Sun

First we'll fly by the biggest, hottest, brightest object in the solar system—the Sun.

Dear Mom ✞ Dad,
    Did ⓤ know that ℝ Sun is really a ☆? It is only a medium-sized ☆, but over ① million Earths could fit inside. We can't 🐝 ② close because of the intense heat (_millions of degrees!_).
    Stay cool— Your ☀ Ray

Mr. +Mrs. Sol Corona
93 Shady Lane
Sun Valley, Idaho
U.S.A.   83353

SOLAR ECLIPSE

I am a STAR!

P.S. The Sun has darker, cooler blotches called SUNSPOTS.

crater

The bowl-shaped holes on a planet or moon are called CRATERS.

Wow! MERCURY is covered with them.

Mercury

Dear Uncle Freddy,
   GUESS THE PLANET—
1) It's closest to the Sun.
2) It has the shortest year (88 Earth days.)
3) It has no water, no air, and no moons.

If you said Mercury, you're right! Also, it is burning hot on the sunny side, and freezing cold on the dark side. Good-bye for now!
   Your nephew,
   Eric

Freddy Fickle
100 Quicksilver Dr.
Frozenfire, Alaska
99552

I'm hot & cold at the same time!

Sunlight

341

Venus

Dear Debbie,
  We saw Venus today,
and it's a little smaller
than Earth, but much
more dangerous. It is
covered with thick, poisonous,
acid clouds. The air has
enough heat and pressure to
crack spaceships! Venus
has lots of earsplitting
thunder, and lightning, too.
  Wish you were here!
      Your friend,
        Simon

Debbie DeMilo
201 Flytrap St.
Cupid City, NY
        12420

VENUS is the second planet from the Sun, and it rotates backwards compared to the other planets.

It looks scary down on the surface.

It's a good thing we sent a robot camera to film it.

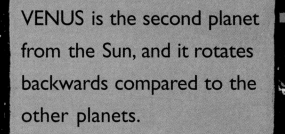

Moon

Dear Mom,
    Guess what? We saw the
actual footprints of the first
astronaut to walk on Earth's
moon~Neil Armstrong. We left
our footprints, too.   They'll
last forever because there's
no wind or rain to destroy them.
I guess a meteor might crash
down on them. That's how the
moon's craters were made. I
hope a meteor doesn't land on us!
            Love,
                Tanisha
P.S. On Earth I weigh 72 pounds-
here I weigh only 12!

Luna Cee
100 Crescent Ave.
Crater Lake, OR
U.S.A. 97604

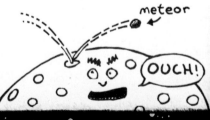

Earth

345

Dear Uncle Martin,
   Here is a poem about Mars~
<u>RED PLANET</u>
   Canyons,
   Volcanoes,
   Clouds of dust,
   Boulders,
   Craters,
   The color of rust.
Scientists think Mars
used to have water in
rivers or oceans. It still
has ice at the poles, but
it's a desert planet now.
   See you! Love,
         Lin

P.S. Mars has 2
small moons.

PHOBOS
DEIMOS

Mr. Martin Greenman
#4 Canal Street
Venice, FL
U.S.A.   33595

I am so
thirsty!

Look at the thousands of asteroids we're passing. The asteroid belt is between the small, rocky inner planets and the giant outer planets.

asteroid

Dear Mom and Dad,
Dr. Quasar says that asteroids are big chunks of rock. Most of them stay in the asteroid belt, but one could drift out of orbit and crash into a planet (even Earth!).
Love,
Simon
P.S. Don't bother wearing helmets— the chance of an asteroid hitting Earth is very small.

Mr. and Mrs. Goldbloom
1000 Collision Road
Bumpers, NJ
U.S.A. 08857

THE ASTEROID BELT

Oh no!

EARTH

JUPITER is made of gases and liquids that swirl around. It has the GREAT RED SPOT, which is really a huge storm.

Dear Stella,
   Did U know that Jupiter is the BIGGEST planet? It has colorful stripes, + a very faint ring system made of dust.  think the weirdest thing is that 🪐 has no solid crust of land. Maybe it is sort of like melted 🍦! Ⓒ U later... Your bro,
Ray
P.S. 🪐 has 16 ☾'s.

Stella Corona
93 Shady Lane
Sun Valley, Idaho
U.S.A. 83353

Jupiter

Saturn

Uranus

Most planets orbit the Sun upright, but URANUS lies on its side.

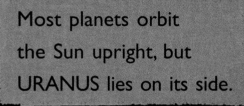

Dear Grandpa & Grandma,
   Uranus is the tilted planet. It looks like a spinning top that fell down. Scientists think a big asteroid could have knocked it over. The whole planet is covered by a thick, blue-green fog. Uranus has rings, just like the other gas giant planets. Also, it has 15 known moons.
   I miss you! Love,
      Tanisha

Mr. and Mrs. Lean
501 Topple St.
Sideways, MI
U.S.A. 48756

353

Pluto

Here is PLUTO, the outermost planet.

The Sun looks so tiny from here!

That's why the outer planets are so cold.

Dear Grandfather,
  Can you believe it—we are 6 billion kilometers from home! Pluto is the very smallest planet, and the last one in the solar system (as far as we know). Scientists think another planet could be hiding out here. Maybe when I grow up, I'll discover it!
  See you soon- Love,
      MINDA
P.S. Pluto has one big moon, called Charon.

PLANET X?

Joe Thunderhawk
248 Final Trail
Tail End, TX
U.S.A. 77050

It's cold out here!

Charon

It's time to head back to Earth. I hope you all enjoyed your tour of the solar system.

Dear Mom + Dad,
   Here R some of the
space words 👁 learned:
ASTEROID- 🪨 space rock
COMET- ☄ chunk of frozen gas & dust
CRATER- ⌣ circular hollow
GALAXY- 🌀 huge group of stars
MOON- 🌑 it orbits a planet
ORBIT- ⟲ to travel around
PLANET- 🪐 it orbits a star
ROTATE- ⟳ to spin
STAR- ☀ it gives off heat and light
👁 want to visit another galaxy next, okay? ♡ Ray

Mr. + Mrs. Sol Corona
93 Shady Lane
Sun Valley, ID
U.S.A. 83353

Think About It

1. What new facts did you learn about the solar system?
2. If possible, which planet would you most like to explore? Why?
3. Why do you think the author chose to give facts about the solar system in the postcards?

Meet the Author and Illustrator
Loreen Leedy

Dear Reader,

When I wrote "Postcards from Pluto," I read many books about our solar system. Then I chose the facts I thought were the most important. The facts had to fit on postcards like this one.

I drew the pictures for this story, too. When I make a book, I write for a while and then I draw for a while. If I change the words, I may have to change the pictures. If I change the pictures, I may have to change the words.

From my home in Florida, I can watch the space shuttle blast off from the space center. It's an inspiring sight! Maybe someday I will watch YOU go into outer space!

Best wishes,

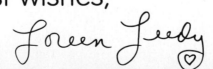

357

GUIDE TO THE SOLAR SYSTEM

Astronaut Neil Armstrong landed on Earth's moon in 1969.

The temperature on Venus climbs to 900 degrees.

Because of how it's tilted, a Mercury day is almost as long as an Earth year!

The Sun's temperature reaches 27 million degrees! The Sun is a star, not a planet.

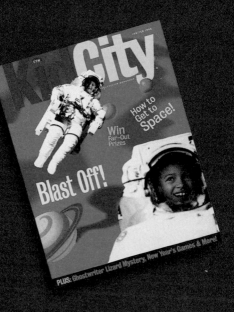

KidCity

How to Get to Space!

Win Far-Out Prizes

Blast Off!

PLUS: Ghostwriter Lizard Mystery, New Year's Games & More!

Jupiter is more than $1\frac{1}{2}$ times larger than all the planets put together.

Pluto is a big ball of frozen gases, water and dirt!

At any time, one side of Uranus is completely dark for 42 days. The other side has 42 days of sunlight!

Neptune is so far from Earth, you can't see it without a telescope.

NASA's Rover landed on Mars in the summer of 1997 and sent back awesome pictures.

Saturn is circled by colorful rings made of ice. Some pieces of ice are as small as fingernails. Others are as big as houses!

LOST IN SPACE?

Can't remember the names of the nine planets? Here's a sentence to help out: My Very Excellent Mom Just Served Us Nice Pickles.

The first letter of each word matches the first letter of each planet—Mercury, Venus, Earth, Mars, Jupiter, Saturn, Uranus, Neptune and Pluto. Get it? Good! We "planet" that way!

THINK ABOUT IT

How else can you remember facts about our solar system?

RESPONSE ACTIVITIES

PLANET FACTS Make fact cards

You can make planet trading cards.

1. Find out more facts about the planets. Look in an encyclopedia **CD-ROM** or in your science book.

2. Write each fact on an index card.

3. On the back of each card, draw a picture about the fact.

Trade your **Planet Cards** with classmates.

Pluto

Sunlight takes about 8 minutes to get to Earth.

Saturn

Moon

GOOD ANSWER! Make a book

Work with a group to make a question-and-answer book about the solar system. Each group member can write one page.

1. Make a list of questions about the solar system.

2. Each group member should choose one question to answer.

3. Write the question at the top of a sheet of paper.

4. Use your science book or an encyclopedia **CD-ROM** to find the answer. Write the answer below the question. Then, draw a picture to show the answer.

5. Put everyone's pages together, and write a title for your book.

Share your question-and-answer book with classmates.

What is the largest moon in the solar system?
The largest moon is Ganymede. It orbits Jupiter.

An Adventure Log

CHARACTER STUDY All of the characters in this theme have adventures. Imagine that you are one of the characters, and keep a journal about your adventure. What would Montigue write about being swallowed by the fish? What would Ruth Law write about flying her plane? Share your journal with your classmates.

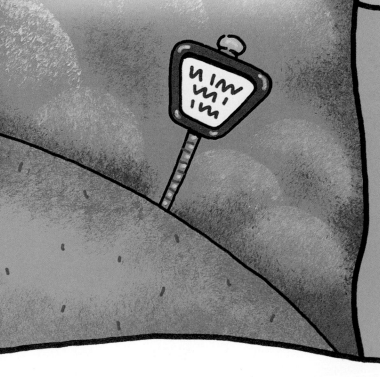

Wish You Were Here

CREATE A POSTCARD Choose a setting from one of the stories in this theme that you would like to visit. Create your own postcard. On a sheet of paper, draw a picture of yourself in this setting. Then turn the paper over. Write a short letter to a classmate about your trip to this place. Deliver your postcard to a classmate and tell why you chose that story.

Literature Circle

DISCUSS THE LITERATURE Get together with a few classmates to talk about the stories in this theme. Read a part from your favorite story. Be ready to tell why you chose that part to read.

Using the Glossary

Get to Know It!

The **Glossary** gives the meaning of a word as it is used in the story. It also gives an example sentence that shows how to use the word. A **synonym**, which is a word that has the same meaning, a **base word**, or **additional word forms** may come after the example sentence. The words in the **Glossary** are in ABC order, also called **alphabetical order**.

Learn to Use It!

If you want to find *oceans* in the **Glossary**, you should first find the *O* words. *O* is near the middle of the alphabet, so the *O* words are near the middle of the **Glossary**. Then you can use the guide words at the top of the page to help you find the entry word *oceans*. It is on page 371.

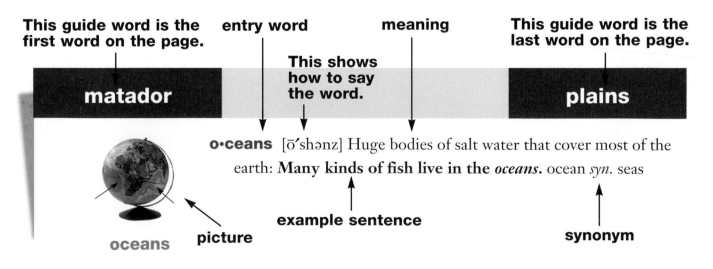

This guide word is the first word on the page.

entry word

meaning

This guide word is the last word on the page.

This shows how to say the word.

matador

plains

o·ceans [ō′shənz] Huge bodies of salt water that cover most of the earth: **Many kinds of fish live in the *oceans*.** ocean *syn.* seas

oceans

picture

example sentence

synonym

A

ad·dress·es [ə•dres′əz] The information on pieces of mail telling whom the mail is for and where those people live: **Make sure the** *addresses* **on the envelopes are correct so the people will get the letters.** address

ad·mired [ad•mīrd′] Liked something or someone: **Sarah's classmates** *admired* **the nice card she had made.** admire, admiring

a·greed [ə•grēd′] Decided together; felt the same way about something: **My brother and I** *agreed* **to share the cookies.** agree, agreeing

ap·peared [ə•pird′] Came into sight: **The rabbit ran into a hole, but it** *appeared* **again a few minutes later.** appear, appearing

as·sem·bled [ə•sem′bəld] Put together from parts or pieces: **The new seesaw had to be** *assembled* **before we could play on it.** assemble, assembling

addresses

B

bor·ing [bôr′ing] Not interesting: **Some stories are exciting, but that story is** *boring*.

C

cap·tured [kap′chərd] Caught and held by someone: **The horse that ran away was** *captured* **and brought back to the barn.** capture, capturing

clasp

clerk

conductor

cas·sette [kə•set´] A case holding a spool of tape for putting into a tape recorder or player: **We listened to my favorite *cassette* tape.**

caused [kôzd] Made something happen: **He jumped up so fast that he *caused* the chair to fall over.** cause, causing

clasp [klasp] A small piece that holds the ends of something together: **She opened the *clasp* on her necklace and took the necklace off.**

clerk [klûrk] A person who sells things in a store: **The *clerk* at the market took my money and gave me my change.**

com·pan·ions [kəm•pan´yənz] People who spend time together: **My *companions* and I play in the park almost every day.** companion

con·duc·tor [kən•duk´tər] The person who helps the people riding on a train: **The *conductor* called out each stop so people would know when to get off the train.**

con·fused [kən•fyo͞ozd´] Mixed up; not sure of what is happening: **Jim felt *confused* by all the traffic and noise in the big city.**

cor·nered [kôr´nərd] Trapped, as if in a corner from which one cannot escape: **It looked as if the dog had the cat *cornered*, but it got away.**

cour·age [kûr´ij] Strength to face danger without fear: **John's little brother showed a lot of *courage* as he rode his new bike for the first time.** *syn.* bravery

co·zy [kō´zē] Warm and comfortable: **We put a blanket in the puppy's basket to make it *cozy* for him.** *syn.* snug

cre·at·ed [krē•āt´əd] Used skill or art to make something new: **The children *created* many pictures and stories.** create, creating

dan·ger·ous [dān′jər•əs] Likely to be harmful; not safe: **It is** *dangerous* **to play with matches.**

dap·pled [dap′əld] Having spots or patches of a different color: **The** *dappled* **fawns will lose their white spots when they grow up.**

de·tails [di•tālz′ or dē′tālz] Facts about something: **Tell me the** *details* **of your trip.** detail

dis·ap·point [dis•ə•point′] To make someone feel bad by not doing what they want you to do: **I know it will** *disappoint* **my friend if I don't go to her party.** disappointed, disappointing

drift·ed [drift′əd] Was carried along by water or air: **When Kim let go of the kite string, her kite** *drifted* **away.** drift, drifting

drow·sy [drou′zē] Sleepy: **If I stay up too late, I feel** *drowsy* **the next day.**

ducked [dukt] Got down quickly to keep from being hit by something: **When Jody saw the ball coming, he** *ducked* **so he wouldn't be hit.** duck, ducking

ex·hi·bi·tion [ek•sə•bish′ən] A display that people come to see: **The museum is having an** *exhibition* **of paintings by children.**

ex·tinct [ik•stingkt′] No longer existing: **We saw models of birds that are** *extinct* **at the natural history museum.**

dappled

drowsy

ducked

fleet

glide

guide

feat [fēt] Something that takes a lot of skill and courage: **Climbing the highest mountain in the world is a great *feat*.**

fleet [flēt] A group of ships or boats that sail together: **We saw a *fleet* of sailboats heading out to sea.**

flock [flok] A group of animals or birds that eat or travel together: **A *flock* of about 100 sheep ate grass on the hill.**

for•ci•bly [fôrs′ə•blē] In a strong way against someone's wishes: **The puppy would not come out of the doghouse and had to be *forcibly* removed.**

fussed [fust] Acted upset about something: **The little children *fussed* as they waited in the long line.** fuss, fussing

gen•tle [jent′əl] Soft and easy; not rough: **The eggs won't break if you are *gentle* with them.**

glide [glīd] To move in a smooth way: **Watch the eagle *glide* across the sky.** glided, gliding

grown [grōn] Finished growing: **That cute little puppy has *grown* to become a big dog.** grow, grew, growing

guide [gīd] A person who leads a trip or tour: **The *guide* at the museum told us interesting facts about the dinosaur bones.**

halt [hôlt] A complete stop: **The marching band came to a *halt* after it marched onto the football field.**

har·bor [här′bər] A place where ships can anchor or be protected in a storm. **The ship sailed into the *harbor* after its long trip across the ocean.**

haze [hāz] Misty or dusty air, such as you might see on a very hot day: **We could not see the tops of the tall buildings through the *haze*.**

her·o·ine [her′ə•wən] A woman or girl who has done something brave or special; a woman or girl who is a hero: **Everyone called Molly a *heroine* after she saved the kitten from the pond.**

hon·or [än′ər] A show of pride in someone or something: **We fly the flag in *honor* of our country.**

ho·ri·zon [hə•rīz′ən] The line where the earth seems to meet the sky: **We were already awake when the sun rose over the *horizon*.**

hos·pi·tal·i·ty [hos•pə•tal′ə•tē] A nice way of treating guests: **We like to eat there because the *hospitality* is as good as the food.**

harbor

horizon

i·mag·i·na·tion [i•maj•ə•nā′shən] The thoughts people use to pretend or to make up stories: **The author must have had a great *imagination* to write a story about talking rocks.**

im·i·tat·ed [im′ə•tāt•əd] Copied the way something looked, acted, or sounded: **Jenny *imitated* the dance steps she saw on television.** imitate, imitating

imitated

in·for·ma·tion [in•fər•mā′shən] Facts: **We went to the library for** *information* **about frogs.**

in·tense [in•tens′] Much stronger or greater than normal: **The light was so** *intense* **that we had to cover our eyes.**

land·scape busi·ness [land′skāp biz′nis] A kind of business in which workers make outdoor places look better by adding plants and changing the land: **Workers in a** *landscape business* **need to know a lot about flowers, trees, and other plants.**

launched [lôncht] Moved a boat from land into the water: **The people on the dock cheered when the ship was** *launched* **into the sea.**

light·ning [līt′ning] Sudden flashes of light in the sky during thunderstorms: **First you see** *lightning,* **and then you hear thunder.**

live·ly [līv′lē] Full of life: **Tanya is a** *lively* **girl who likes to be busy all the time.**

loom·ing [loom′ing] Coming into sight looking large and scary: **We saw the old house** *looming* **before us on the dark hill.** loom, loomed

lug·gage [lug′ij] Suitcases and bags used in traveling: **We put our** *luggage* **in the car.**

man·ners [man′ərz] Ways of acting that show that a person is polite: **Children who have good** *manners* **do not play with their food.**

lightning

mat·a·dor [mat′ə•dôr] A person who fights bulls for sport: **The matador waved his red cape as the bull ran around the ring.**

mim·icked [mim′ikt] Copied what someone else said or did: **The boys bent their knees and *mimicked* the funny way the circus clown walked.** mimic, mimicking

mist [mist] Tiny drops of water that hang in the air and make the air look white: **We couldn't see far in the early morning *mist*.**

mist

nev·er [nev′ər] Not at all; not ever: **I live in Florida and have *never* seen snow.**

no·tice [nō′tis] To see or pay attention to: **We didn't *notice* the dark clouds in the sky until it began to rain.** noticed, noticing

oceans

ob·jects [ob′jikts] Things that can be seen or touched: **The bag was filled with small *objects*, such as coins, buttons, and toys.** object

o·ceans [ō′shənz] Huge bodies of salt water that cover most of the earth: **Many kinds of fish live in the *oceans*.** ocean *syn.* seas

pale [pāl] Light in color: **I mixed white paint and green paint to make a *pale* green color.**

plains [plānz] Flat lands with no trees: **The open *plains* stretched ahead of us as far as we could see.**

plains

371

pour [pôr] To move in a steady stream: **Children pour out the school's front door when the bell rings.** poured, pouring

R

ranch [ranch] A kind of large farm where cows, horses, or sheep are raised: **It took the cowhands all day to move the cattle from one part of the *ranch* to another.**

ranch

re·al·ized [rē′ə•līzd] Came to understand something: **After a few tries, the boys *realized* that they needed a longer rope.** realize, realizing

re·flects [ri•flekts′] Gives back light that shines on it: **The moon *reflects* the sunlight that shines on it.** reflect, reflected, reflecting

re·fused [ri•fyoozd′] Did not do what was asked: **Mother *refused* to give us ice cream before dinner.** refuse, refusing

rel·a·tives [rel′ə•tivz] People in the same family: **My aunts, uncles, cousins, and other *relatives* came to the party.** relative

re·lax [ri•laks′] Take a rest: **After playing ball, we like to sit down and *relax*.** relaxed, relaxing

relax

re·moves [ri•moovz′] Takes something off: **He *removes* his shoes and puts on his slippers.** remove, removed, removing

rhythm [rith′əm] A set of sounds repeated again and again: **We clapped our hands to the *rhythm* of the music.**

roamed [rōmd] Moved around in many directions: **Our lost dog *roamed* for days before we found her.** roam, roaming

route [root or rout] The path that a salesperson or delivery person always follows: **Our newspaper carrier follows her *route* every day.**

372

sense [sens] A correct way of thinking: **It makes *sense* to wear a helmet when you ride a bike.**

soared [sôrd] Flew high into the air: **The bird *soared* high above the earth on its strong wings.** soar, soaring

spec·ta·tors [spek′tā·tərz] People who watch something: **The *spectators* cheered when the batter hit a home run.** spectator *syn.* onlookers

star·tled [stärt′əld] Surprised and frightened: **The sudden noise *startled* me and made me drop my cup.** startle, startling

still [stil] Quiet: **Everyone was asleep, and the house was *still*.** *syn.* silent

stood [sto͝od] Stayed the same: **The record for the most home runs *stood* for many years.** stand, standing

stroke [strōk] Rub in a gentle way: **My cat likes it when I *stroke* her back.** stroked, stroking

stur·dy [stûr′dē] Strong: **The little tree grew to be tall and *sturdy*.**

sup·pose [sə·pōz′] To think something is likely: **Dad's car is in the driveway, so I *suppose* he must be home.** supposed, supposing

sur·face [sûr′fəs] The outside or the top of something: **The *surface* of a watermelon is green, but the inside is red.**

swoop·ing [swo͞op′ing] Coming down in a wide, curving movement: **The hawk was *swooping* down from the sky.** swoop, swooped

spectators

stroke

thou·sands [thouz′andz] Many, many hundreds: **There are** *thousands* **of leaves on that big oak tree.** thousand

typ·i·cal [tip′i•kəl] Very much like other things of the same kind: **A** *typical* **school day includes reading and math lessons.**

va·ca·tion [vā•kā′shən] Time off from school or work: **When summer** *vacation* **is over, it's time to go back to school.**

vet·er·i·nar·i·an [vet•ər•ə•när′ē•ən] A doctor who treats animals: **Kelly took her sick dog to a** *veterinarian*.

Index of Authors

Page numbers in color tell where you can read about the author.

Acknowledgments

For permission to reprint copyrighted material, grateful acknowledgment is made to the following sources:

Aladdin Paperbacks, an imprint of Simon & Schuster Children's Publishing Division: Cover illustration from *Regards to the Man in the Moon* by Ezra Jack Keats. Copyright © 1981 by Ezra Jack Keats.

Atheneum Books for Young Readers, Simon & Schuster Children's Publishing Division: Cover illustration by David S. Rose from *There's a Dragon in My Sleeping Bag* by James Howe. Illustration copyright © 1994 by David S. Rose.

Boyds Mills Press, Inc.: Cover illustration by Maryann Cocca-Leffler from *Wanda's Roses* by Pat Brisson. Illustration copyright © 1994 by Maryann Cocca-Leffler.

Curtis Brown Ltd.: "Last Laugh" from *Blast Off: Poems About Space* by Lee Bennett Hopkins. Text copyright © 1974 by Lee Bennett Hopkins. Published by HarperCollins Publishers.

Children's Television Workshop, New York, NY: From "Cool It!" by Lynn O'Donnell in *3-2-1 Contact Magazine*, July/August 1997. Text copyright 1997 by Children's Television Workshop. From "Birds Do It! Recycle!" in *Kid City Magazine*, April 1995. Text © 1995 by Children's Television Workshop. From "Operation Space Station" (Retitled: "Guide to the Solar System") in *Kid City Magazine*, January/February 1998. Text © 1997 by Children's Television Workshop.

Clarion Books/Houghton Mifflin Company: Cover illustration by David Wisniewski from *Ducky* by Eve Bunting. Illustration copyright © 1997 by David Wisniewski. *Anthony Reynoso: Born to Rope* by Martha Cooper and Ginger Gordon. Text copyright © 1996 by Ginger Gordon; photographs copyright © 1996 by Martha Cooper.

Crown Publishers, Inc.: From *How I Spent My Summer Vacation* by Mark Teague. Copyright © 1995 by Mark Teague.

Dial Books for Young Readers, a division of Penguin Putnam Inc.: From *Snakey Riddles* by Katy Hall and Lisa Eisenberg, illustrated by Simms Taback. Text copyright © 1990 by Katy Hall and Lisa Eisenberg; illustrations copyright © 1990 by Simms Taback. *The Day Jimmy's Boa Ate the Wash* by Trinka Hakes Noble, illustrated by Steven Kellogg. Text copyright © 1980 by Trinka Hakes Noble; illustrations copyright © 1980 by Steven Kellogg.

Dutton Children's Books, a division of Penguin Putnam Inc.: *Abuela* by Arthur Dorros, illustrated by Elisa Kleven. Text copyright © 1991 by Arthur Dorros; illustrations copyright © 1991 by Elisa Kleven. Cover illustration from *The Puddle Pail* by Elisa Kleven. Copyright © 1997 by Elisa Kleven.

Greenwillow Books, a division of William Morrow & Company, Inc.: Cover illustration by Barry Root from *Grandpa Takes Me to the Moon* by Timothy R. Gaffney. Illustration copyright © 1996 by Barrett V. Root. *Good-bye, Curtis* by Kevin Henkes, illustrated by Marisabina Russo. Text copyright © 1995 by Kevin Henkes; illustrations copyright © 1995 by Marisabina Russo.

Harcourt Brace & Company: Cover illustration from *Out of the Ocean* by Debra Frasier. Copyright © 1998 by Debra Frasier.

Florence Parry Heide: Lyrics by Florence Parry Heide from "Wheels" in *Songs to Sing About Things You Think About.* Lyrics © 1971 by Florence Parry Heide.

Holiday House, Inc.: *Postcards from Pluto: A Tour of the Solar System* by Loreen Leedy. Copyright © 1993 by Loreen Leedy.

Houghton Mifflin Company: Cover illustration from *Author: A True Story* by Helen Lester. Copyright © 1997 by Helen Lester. *Ruth Law Thrills a Nation* by Don Brown. Copyright © 1993 by Don Brown.

Kane/Miller Book Publishers: *The Park Bench* by Fumiko Takeshita, illustrated by Mamoru Suzuki. Copyright © by Fumiko Takeshita/Mamoru Suzuki; American text copyright © 1988 by Kane/Miller Book Publishers.

Little, Brown and Company: From *Dinosaurs Travel* by Laurie Krasny Brown and Marc Brown. Copyright © 1988 by Laurie Krasny Brown and Marc Brown.

Margaret K. McElderry Books, Simon & Schuster Children's Publishing Division: Dear Mr. Blueberry by Simon James. Copyright © 1991 by Simon James. Originally published in Great Britain by Walker Books, Ltd. *Cool Ali* by Nancy Poydar. Copyright © 1996 by Nancy Poydar.

North-South Books, Inc., New York: Cover photograph from *On an Island in the Bay* by Patricia Mills. Copyright © 1994 by Patricia Mills.

Orchard Books, New York: Cover illustration by David Soman from *The Leaving Morning* by Angela Johnson. Illustration copyright © 1992 by David Soman.

Simon & Schuster Books for Young Readers, an imprint of Simon & Schuster Children's Publishing Division: Cover illustration by Brian Pinkney from *Where Does the Trail Lead?* by Burton Albert. Illustration copyright © 1991 by Brian Pinkney. Cover illustration by Robert Casilla from *The Little Painter of Sabana Grande* by Patricia Maloney Markun. Illustration copyright © 1993 by Robert Casilla. Cover illustration from *Six-Dinner Sid* by Inga Moore. Copyright © 1991 by Inga Moore. *Max Found Two Sticks* by Brian Pinkney. Copyright © 1994 by Brian Pinkney. *It's Probably Good Dinosaurs Are Extinct* by Ken Raney. Copyright © 1993 by Ken Raney. Cover illustration by Byron Barton from *Gila Monsters Meet You at the Airport* by Marjorie Weinman Sharmat. Illustration copyright © 1980 by Byron Barton.

Troll Communications L.L.C.: Cover illustration by Dennis Davidson from *The Sun and Other Stars* by Richard Harris. Illustration copyright © 1996 by Dennis Davidson.

William Van Clief: Music by Sylvia Worth Van Clief from "Wheels" in *Songs to Sing About Things You Think About.* Music © 1971 by Sylvia Worth Van Clief.

Viking Penguin, a division of Penguin Putnam Inc.: *Montigue On the High Seas* by John Himmelman. Copyright © 1988 by John Himmelman.

Photo Credits

Key: (t)=top, (b)=bottom, (c)=center, (l)=left, (r)=right
Courtesy, Walker Books, 79; Pamela Zilly / The Image Bank, 126; G. C. Kelly/FPG, 127(t); Jim Cummins/FPG, 127(c); Jeffrey Sylvester/FPG, 127(b); Rod Planck/ Photo Researchers, 128(t); Anthony Merceca/Photo Researchers, 128(c); John Cancalosi/Tom Stack & Associates, 128(b); John Gerlach/Tom Stack & Associates, 129(l); Renee Lynn/Photo Researchers, 129(r); Mike Woodside, 171(r); Roger Wilmshurst/Bruce Coleman, Inc., 172(t); (sky) Joseph Nettis/Photo Researchers, 172(b); (boy) Jade Albert, 172(b); Martha Cooper, 220-234; Jim Norman, 235(l); Martha Cooper, 235(r); Kindra Clineff/The Picture Cube, 366(b); Stephen J. Krasemann/Photo Researchers, 367(t); The Stock Market, 367(b); Daniel J. Cox/ Tony Stone Images, 368(t); Joseph Nettis/Stock, Boston, 368(b); Jose Fuste Rada/ The Stock Market, 369(t); Herb Schmitz / Tony Stone Images, 369(b); Spencer Swanger/Tom Stack & Associates, 370; Ronald W. Weir/The Stock Market, 371(t); Ken Martin/Visuals Unlimited, 371(b); D.R. Stocklein/The Stock Market, 372; Charles Krebs/The Stock Market, 373(t); Claude Charlier/The Stock Market, 373(b).
All other photos by Harcourt:
Peter Finge /Black Star, Chuck Kneyse/Black Star, Rick Friedman/Black Star, Walt Chrynwski/Black Star, Mark Derse/Black Star, Tom Sobolik/Black Star, Peter Silvia/Black Star, Joseph Rupp/Black Star, Dale Higgins, Ron Kunzman, Ken Kenzie, Victoria Bowen, Terry Sinclair.

Illustration Credits

Diane Greenseid, Cover Art; Gary Taxali, 2-3, 10-11, 12-13, 132-133; Will Terry, 4-5, 134-135, 136-137, 240-241; Jennifer Beck-Harris, 6-7, 242-243, 244-245, 362-363; Steven Kellogg, 14-31, 34-35; Simms Tabak, 32-33; Mark Teague, 36-53, 54-55; Dave Herrick, 56-57; Simon James, 58-79, 82-83; Michael Maydak, 80-81; Ken Raney, 84-105, 106-107; Katy Farmer, 108-109; Nancy Poydar, 110-125, 126-127; Mamoru Suzuki, 138-153, 154-155; Mary GrandPré, 156-171, 174-175; Marisabina Russo, 176-193, 194-195; Billy Davis, 196-197, 238-239; Brian Pinkney, 198-217, 218-219; Ginger Gordon, 220-235, 236-237; John Himmelman, 246-259, 260-261; Cathy Bennett, 262-263; Marc Brown, 264-283, 286-287; Nancy Davis, 284-285; Elisa Kleven, 288-307, 308-309; Tuko Fujisaki, 310-311; Don Brown, 312-329, 332-333; Nancy Coffelt, 330-331; Loreen Leedy, 334-357, 360-361; Holly Cooper, 367, 368, 369, 372